within
SMALL HOMES

PAGE ONE

Within Small Homes
© 2003 Page One Publishing Private Limited

Published by
Page One Publishing Private Limited
20 Kaki Bukit View
Kaki Bukit Techpark II
Singapore 415956
Tel: 65-6742 2088
Fax: 65-6744 2088
Email: pageone@singnet.com.sg

Editorial Coordination & Text (in alphabetical order):
Anna Koor (Hong Kong, China)
Barbara Cullen (Melbourne, Australia)
Meng-Ching Kwah (Tokyo, Japan)
Reiko Kasai (Tokyo, Japan)
Richard Se (Kuala Lumpur, Malaysia)
Savinee Buranasilapin (Bangkok, Thailand)
Tatsuo Iso (Tokyo, Japan)
Thomas Dannecker (Bangkok, Thailand)

Designers:
Chai-Yen Wong
Sharn Selina Lim

Sub-Editors/Writers:
Hwee-Chuin Ang
Narelle Yabuka

Art Director:
Jacinta Neoh

Editorial Director:
Kelley Cheng

Colour Separation:
SC Graphic Technology Pte Ltd

Printer:
Stampa Nazionale s.r.l., Italy

Printed in Italy
ISBN: 981-4019-94-1

On the cover
Design by Peter Tay/POM (Singapore)
Photography by Geoff Ang / Courtesy of ISH magazine

within
SMALL HOMES

PAGE ONE

contents

008 introduction

010 albert park house | NICHOLAS GIOIA ARCHITECTS australia

018 fitzroy terrace | SHELLEY PENN ARCHITECTS australia

026 richardson street house | NICHOLAS GIOIA ARCHITECTS australia

032 richmond warehouse | SHELLEY PENN ARCHITECTS australia

040 south melbourne house | NICHOLAS GIOIA ARCHITECTS australia

048 apartment in south bay | AB CONCEPT LTD hong kong

054 artist's residence | DRAUGHTZMAN hong kong

064 bachelor residence | AFSO DESIGN hong kong

072 bertrand / lee apartment | ONE: CHINA STUDIO hong kong

080 gary's apartment | EDGE (HK) LTD hong kong

088 ken rose apartment | ARCHITUDE STUDIO hong kong

094 paul hicks apartment | BHI LTD hong kong

102 peak apartment | KplusK ASSOCIATES hong kong

112 shama apartment 1 | DILLON GARRIS hong kong

120 shama apartment 2 | DILLON GARRIS hong kong

126 wong apartment | SUNAQUA CONCEPTS LTD hong kong

134 9 tubo house | MAKOTO KOIZUMI japan

144 beaver house | AKIRA YONEDA & MASAHIRO IKEDA japan

152 borzoi house | N MAEDA ATELIER japan

160 c house | TELE-DESIGN COLLABORATIVE NETWORK japan

168 hachijo atelier | NORIHIKO DAN AND ASSOCIATES japan

176 house at matsubara | SATOSHI OKADA ARCHITECTS japan

184 house in mount fuji | SATOSHI OKADA ARCHITECTS japan

192 k house lounge | D.M.A japan

200 m house | CLIP japan

208 natural illuminance | EDH ENDOH DESIGN HOUSE + MIAS japan

contents

214 oh house | AKO NAGAO ARCHITECT OFFICE japan

222 rooftecture m | SHUHEI ENDO ARCHITECT INSTITUTE japan

230 screen house at senkawa | ARCHITECT CAFE japan

238 studio yukobo | FORMS japan

246 t-set | CHIBA MANABU ARCHITECTS japan

254 damansara perdana | ZLG SDN BHD malaysia

260 house at bukit antarabangsa | PH+D DESIGN malaysia

270 timber house at batu laut | C'ARCH ARCHITECTURE + DESIGN SDN BHD malaysia

278 commonwealth avenue west | WIDE OPEN SPACES singapore

286 figaro street | CU FUA ASSOCIATES singapore

294 fortredale apartment | WHIZ CONCEPTS singapore

300 ghim moh flat | WHIZ CONCEPTS singapore

308 house at jalan bahagia | ZONG ARCHITECTS singapore

316 kim tian road apartment | WHIZ CONCEPTS singapore

326 lengkong tiga apartment | WHIZ CONCEPTS singapore

334 moulmein road apartment | THE MATCHBOX singapore

342 oxley rise apartment | WEAVE INTERIOR singapore

348 punggol road apartment | CU FUA ASSOCIATES singapore

356 telok blangah apartment | WARREN LIU & DARLENE SMYTH singapore

366 ban suan saghob | ARCHITECTS 49 LTD thailand

374 beaux house | PICHAI-THEERANUJ WONGWAISAYAWAN thailand

382 gerd fabritius condo | P INTERIOR & ASSOCIATES CO., LTD thailand

390 osataphan residence | ARCHITECTS 49 LTD / IA ARCHITECTS 49 LIMITED thailand

398 index

400 acknowledgments

introduction

As our cities become more populated and dense, our dwelling spaces are becoming smaller and smaller. In the most crowded of cities, such as Hong Kong or Tokyo, an entire apartment may only be the size of a single room in a more spacious home elsewhere. Such spatial restriction, of course, requires of the architect or designer a great deal of innovation.

The homes presented in this book may be restricted in square footage, but they are unlimited in terms of innovation, style and practicality. They show exciting new ways to conceptualise and configure spaces within small homes for ultimate flexibility and full maximisation of space. With rich colour photographs and descriptive and analytical text, Within Small Homes showcases fifty small homes from around the Asia and Pacific region, which range from a tiny 330 square foot apartment in Hong Kong, to a Mies van der Rohe-inspired architect's house situated in a lush forest outside Bangkok. Reflective of new ways of living, these homes range widely in type - from free-standing dwellings, apartments, terrace houses and shophouses, to recycled spaces such as converted industrial warehouses and medical clinics. Varied in type they may be, but lacking in innovation they are not.

The benefits of small homes are many; besides having a lower purchase price, they have greater ease of upkeep, they use less energy and they can be decidedly cosy. Compact and efficient, these small homes offer terrific inspiration for the maximisation of space in the small home, and illustrate ingenious methods for dividing space, configuring storage, and using lighting and furnishings to the greatest advantage. Within Small Homes shows, above all, that bigger does not necessarily mean better.

DIVISIBLE BY 2

albert park house

An extension to an existing single storey weatherboard Edwardian house was an exercise in tight, dense planning. A severe orthogonal idiom has created what is, in effect, a new house co-existing alongside the old.

PROJECT LOCATION **MELBOURNE, AUSTRALIA**
FLOOR AREA **2152SQFT**
ARCHITECT/DESIGNER **NICHOLAS GIOIA, RODGER SMITH, NICHOLAS DOUR/NICHOLAS GIOIA ARCHITECTS**
PHOTOGRAPHER **TREVOR MEIN**
TEXT **NARELLE YABUKA**

Before the renovation, this house comprised two distinct parts. The front half was single storey Edwardian in a reasonable condition, but it was very dark and gloomy. The back half, a "modern" addition, was a disaster. Although it was built barely 10 years ago, it was already virtually dilapidated. Furthermore, this single storey addition was crudely and illogically designed. Even after the renovation, the house comprises two distinct parts – and deliberately so. The brief stipulated that the house should encompass two elements making up one whole. The renovation does exactly that, but the change has been vast.

The Edwardian front half of the house has been inexpensively restored. This part of the house includes the master bedroom, guest bedroom, formal sitting room and a study. It is the quiet and rather formal part of the house, which also allows the owners a backdrop for their pre-20th Century furniture. The modern rear half of the house is 2-storey high and completely different from the front. The ground floor comprises the kitchen, dining and living areas and also the main bathroom, the laundry and the en suite to the master bedroom. The upper level comprises children's bedrooms, another bathroom, a recreation area, and, believe it or not, a "cellar". It is probably the only "cellar" in Australia on an upper floor, but it does work!

The language of this addition is modern. The owners say that it is well planned, and it definitely has presence. Although this rear half is 2-storey high, it is not at all visible from the street. Similarly, the Edwardian front half is not visible from the rear garden. This was a deliberate strategy – the creation of two houses within one – and it has given the owners the two types of residence they desired.

FLUID VOLUMES

fitzroy terrace house

The fall of a long, narrow site has facilitated a fluid unfolding of volumes extending from an existing terrace house.

PROJECT LOCATION **MELBOURNE, AUSTRALIA**
ARCHITECT/DESIGNER **SHELLEY PENN ARCHITECT**
PHOTOGRAPHER **PETER CLARKE/COURTESY OF SHELLEY PENN ARCHITECTS**
TEXT **NARELLE YABUKA**

This project involved alterations and extensions to an existing terrace house in inner urban Melbourne. The site is long and narrow, at 40 x 4.5 metres, and has a substantial fall towards the rear. The house is sandwiched between two tall structures. The front section of the house has been relatively untouched, with only a new fence, front door and garden subtly indicating that some change has been made. Moving through the building, the spaces step down with the site and the whole unfolds from a typical small row house to reveal a series of fluid volumes that open the space to the back garden and the sky.

The ground floor spaces are lit by reflected and filtered light that enters through skylights between ceiling planes and windows. These skylights cut across the direction of travel, creating rhythm and occasions for pause in movement. At first floor level, there is a studio and sun deck, which are reached via a narrow, somewhat mysterious stair. They are set low amongst the rooftops, the intention being to create intimate and private spaces rather than attempting to capture views. In this case, the spaces are flooded by natural light in contrast to the relative seclusion below.

In this tightly planned series of small spaces, fluid volumes are created in response to the chasm-like landscape of the original site, and light and passage are used to order the experience.

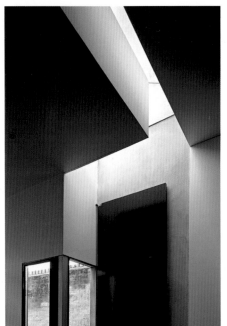

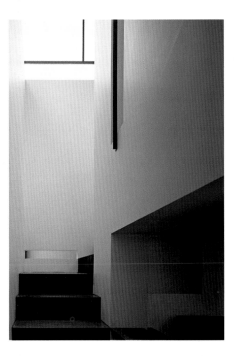

NAUGHTS AND CROSSES

richardson street house

Restraint and elegance were the defining principles for the renovation of this old house, but some sculptural fenestration has given it a fresh expressiveness.

PROJECT LOCATION **MELBOURNE, AUSTRALIA**
FLOOR AREA **2454SQFT**
ARCHITECT/DESIGNER **NICHOLAS GIOIA, PATRICK GILFEDDER/NICHOLAS GIOIA ARCHITECTS**
PHOTOGRAPHER **TREVOR MEIN**
TEXT **NARELLE YABUKA**

The house is located in a part of Albert Park that was developed in the latter part of the 19th Century. The street is wide, but still the site feels very hemmed in. The site is small relative to the size of both the existing dwelling and the modified dwelling. The building has been designed to take full advantage of the site in terms of creating as much interior space as possible, allowing views onto landscaped areas and letting in controllable sunlight. Despite a significant amount of enclosed space, the addition is very compact and "contained", and therefore does not bear down on its neighbours.

The notions that formed the basis of the design are restraint, precision, simplicity and elegance. The organisation of spaces and functions both externally and internally is very simple and obvious. The owner wanted the bedrooms to face the street and the living areas to face a private outdoor living area. As a result, the bathroom and laundry are in the middle, and the kitchen joins the dining and living rooms at the rear, facing a secluded courtyard that can also accommodate a car when required. The living areas and bathroom also face a second courtyard that cuts into the middle of the house, admitting light generously.

The dining area is double-height, with a terrific feeling of spaciousness. A mezzanine level, enclosed by a low wall, sits above the living, which thus gains a certain level of intimacy. The interior, with its calm palette of white walls and timber floors, is brought to life by two sculptural windows: a gigantic asymmetrical cross on the wall siding the dining, and a round skylight, or naught, above. A circle of light thus elegantly parades its way across the interior during the day, and sleek strips of the sky and the neighbouring property are seen through the dining room.

NEW AND OLD

richmond warehouse

In a quiet corner of post-industrial Richmond, Melbourne, brutal and historic warehouse architecture meets glass-and-metal modernity. Shelley Penn has inserted an objet d'art - physically compact and beguilingly simple - into this unassuming stretch of the neighbourhood.

PROJECT LOCATION **MELBOURNE, AUSTRALIA**
ARCHITECT/DESIGNER **SHELLEY PENN ARCHITECTS**
PHOTOGRAPHER **TREVOR MEIN/COURTESY OF SHELLEY PENN ARCHITECTS**
TEXT **NARELLE YABUKA**

This award-winning project is a stunning example of how the new can be merged with the old. The architect has made a polite addition to the old shell of what was originally one corner of a vinegar factory. This project involved the conversion of a tiny (approximately 7 x 7 x 7 metre) warehouse shell in semi-industrial Richmond, to provide a home and painting studio. The design intention was to respond to the tiny site and small budget with a concise but emotionally rich solution.

With mass brick walls on three sides, and a strong street presence, the approach was to leave the original shell alone and to replace the single timber-framed, east wall with a new 3-dimensional tower-box. In deference to the original east wall, this new form is lightweight, timber-framed and metal-clad. With tenuous connections to the three existing brick boundary walls, it is inserted into the embrace of the original brick shell, with light entering around it. It is tightly packed vertically, and is very small in floor area - housing the intimate functions of ablutions and sleep.

More exuberant activities occur in the remainder of the two original volumes. Circulation occurs in the gaps between the old and new, with the staircase cutting vertical shafts between them. As you spiral up through the building, the relationship between old and new is exposed, and at the same time, progressively more natural light enters while views out increase. The experience culminates in the arrival at an almost precarious projecting balcony, which is fully exposed to the street, the north sun and the landscape of Richmond.

BREAKING DOWN BARRIERS

south melbourne house

This project proposes a refreshing prototype for the rejuvenation of a common inner suburban housing type in Australia - the terrace house. Solving problems to do with a lack of space and outlook, the architects have created a welcoming and restful haven.

PROJECT LOCATION **MELBOURNE, AUSTRALIA**
FLOOR AREA **1065SQFT**
ARCHITECT/DESIGNER **NICHOLAS GIOIA, THOMAS VAKAS/NICHOLAS GIOIA ARCHITECTS**
PHOTOGRAPHER **TREVOR MEIN**
TEXT **NARELLE YABUKA**

With their renovation of this South Melbourne terrace house, Nicholas Gioia Architects have solved some of the common problems of small single-fronted homes, such as narrowness, lack of outlook, claustrophobia and gloom. They have shown that even if such a building is constricted by its neighbours, it can still feel spacious, admit lots of controllable sunlight, have views in many directions, and have an "adaptable" ambience that can range from "cocooning" to exhilarating.

The renovation allows the occupants to experience the exhilaration of spaciousness in a narrow house. It has let in ample sunshine via extensive but protected glazing and discrete, concealed skylights. Futhermore, the renovation has afforded the owners with views out onto three landscaped courtyards. The palette is pared back, with white walls and ceilings interjected by timber storage elements that have specially carved display niches.

The design has turned a less than desirable property into a value-added one that is expected to be much sought after if ever sold. Construction costs were kept down by the use of economical materials and an avoidance of complicated details. Meanwhile, energy consumption is much less than average. All windows are externally shaded to prevent excessive heat gain, and are internally covered to prevent excessive heat loss. Walls and ceilings are insulated to a much greater degree than is required by regulations, and the entire space is heated by one gas heater and two small electric heaters. The design provides a comfortable, practical and easy-to-live-with interior that moderates extremes in temperature, and has impressed neighbours and visitors to rethink the approach to their own homes.

DISPLAY CASE

apartment in south bay

Having lived in their apartment for almost eight years, the owners decided it was time to rethink their living space both aesthetically and in consideration of the growing number of artefacts and *objets d'art* that they had collected over time.

PROJECT LOCATION **SOUTH BAY, HONG KONG**
FLOOR AREA **1500SQFT**
ARCHITECT/DESIGNER **AB CONCEPT LTD**
PHOTOGRAPHER **EDGAR TAPAN**
TEXT **ANNA KOOR**

One of the primary starting points for the designer of this spacious apartment was the owners' passion for crystal glass and the need to display this in an ordered manner. Their collection previously occupied any available horizontal surface, with the result that there was no real focus. By converting the study into a multi-purpose space that also provided acres of storage, the designers were able to resolve several issues at once. The entire floor was raised to create an under-floor storage hold. Hinged doors flip up for access. The open-sided box is like a Japanese pavilion: the owners can entertain here and admire the surrounding displays; a panel opens to reveal a small workstation with all the essential telecommunications equipment; and guests can sleep over - tatami style - by retrieving futon beds from beneath the floor.

The semi-rural neighbourhood prompted the designers to create a more imaginative outlook from their living room that captured a non-urban ambience. An existing deep planter outside the window was converted into a fishpond with a fibreglass basin, and filled with banks of pebbles and rock plants. This micro-landscape is illuminated at night.

Display niches are organised in a graphic format of horizontal slots, set off by targeted lighting and smokey-grey mirror cabinets that float off the floor and blend in with the walls, rather than simply being pieces of furniture. This enhances the forms of the chunky, freestanding furniture, all of which was custom-made by the designers. Its almost primitive qualities are absent of fussy detailing. The smoked mirror - a favourite of the designers - was chosen for its mysterious qualities and soft reflections, which are unlike those of standard mirrors.

SHIFTING PLANES

artist's residence

This artist's apartment contains no computers, telephones or TVs. Instead, this nest for meditation, rest and sleep contains what could be described as a Rubik's Cube in furniture form, with a kitchen that can grow and shrink.

PROJECT LOCATION **MID-LEVELS, HONG KONG**
ARCHITECT/DESIGNER **DRAUGHTZMAN**
PHOTOGRAPHER **KELLEY CHENG**
TEXT **ANNA KOOR**

Evelyna Yee-woo Liang does not appear to be someone who is bound by rules; and the interior of her home, indeed, has no rigid form to it. She can choose to sleep, rest or eat anywhere she likes. If she needs to create something more formal for the times when her family visits, she can partition the space into a separate bedroom. Furthermore, when she entertains, there is one big party room to do it in.

In its previous life, the flat was compartmentalised into a row of three minute bedrooms leading off a dark corridor. One length of the corridor was removed, as well as the intervening walls, to leave one big living space with three windows overlooking the city. In the living room, the sill-ledge is extended back into the space to become a double bed, meditative platform, or a gathering point for tea drinking. The central portion hides a void underneath, which stows a roll-out tatami mat and bedding. It has been delineated by the act of cladding the platform, walls and ceiling in a different material - in this case a wood veneer.

The kitchen no longer takes a huge chunk out of the limited space; it is as small as a cupboard when not in use or almost half the apartment when cooking. One permanent wall cuts across the apartment, which hides the kitchen within a glowing box. Cooking facilities are plugged into the wall on one side, and a display bookshelf is mounted on the reverse. All of this is curtained in frosted citrus glazed panels that concertina back when required. The remaining passageway wall distributes the bathroom amenities and storage. Substituting doors, there are three cement-faced moveable walls that glide across the various openings. One of these panels also swings right out, creating a temporary wall across the apartment when privacy is needed. Each time a panel is moved, a flash of lime green painted on the original wall beneath is revealed. The singular piece of furniture occupying the centre of the room is a stroke of genius. It can be remodelled at any opportunity - for sleeping, eating, studying - or it can be completely "sociable" during a party, when guests can recline on and circulate around it. Its principle is similar to a Rubik's Cube. In its most compact form, it is a rectangular bed with a side table. Deconstruct it and the three pieces are zigzagged in section, ranging from small to large in size, and able to intersect with each other to create social seating.

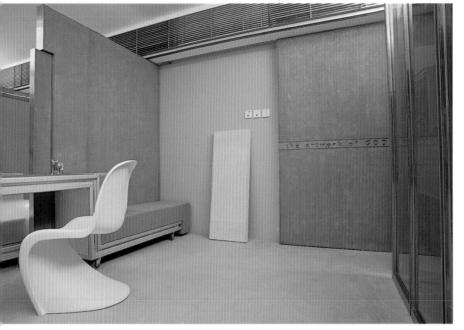

we are   the artwork of GOD

A THEATRICAL MONOLOGUE

bachelor residence

Proportion, light and scale are captured and manipulated in the renovation of this bachelor's apartment. The result is a theatrical space of movement, compression and release.

PROJECT LOCATION **MID-LEVELS, HONG KONG**
FLOOR AREA **930SQFT**
ARCHITECT/DESIGNER **ANDRE FU/AFSO DESIGN**
PHOTOGRAPHER **JOHN BUTLIN & KELLEY CHENG**
TEXT **ANNA KOOR**

The 930 square-foot apartment was formerly partitioned into three bedrooms and two bathrooms distributed from a central corridor, making it exceedingly cramped. The architect's intention was to create an unassuming sanctuary for modern urban living. Fortunately, the absence of structural walls presented the opportunity to open out the space somewhat, and create a panorama of spectacular views, instead of a fragmented outlook. From the entrance, the circulation is orchestrated by a curving passage, which is deliberately compressed and dimly illuminated - a prelude to what lies beyond. The kitchen is tucked into the left-hand corner. A typical layout would normally place the front entrance bang in the living space, so this re-modelling creates a dramatic transition prior to the main event.

The "theatre" is also played out by a wall of sheer drapery covering the peripheral wall, up-lit from the floor. Navigating the constricted corridor accentuates the eventual confrontation with open space as one turns the corner; movement, compression then release using proportion, light and scale. The curved wall also forms the enclosure to the bathroom, toilet and walk-in closet, planned as a procession of intimate spaces that celebrate the daily rituals of washing and dressing.

A symmetrical volume combines living, dining, working and resting functions, oriented so that each can be used simultaneously without disrupting other areas. Equally, there is room for flexibility between different uses. The central bulkhead, which serves as a conduit for lighting, is clad in steel, reducing its mass with its subtle reflectivity. Pietra di Lecce limestone, solid ash furniture and plastered surfaces provide a counterpoint to steel and the smoked glass modesty screen between the end of the bed and the dining table. Accents of pale blue and aubergine form an unusual colour palette. In addition to the sheer curtain, exaggerated swathes of black gloss lacquered cupboards heighten the aspect of scale and volume in a linear mode.

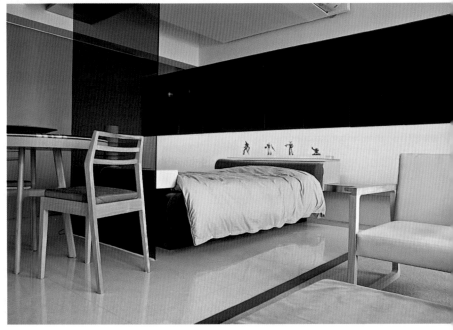

A FOCUSED ARRANGEMENT

bertrand / lee apartment

A new wall that cuts right through this photographer's apartment frames views and pulls spaces into a focused arrangement.

PROJECT LOCATION **MID-LEVELS, HONG KONG**
FLOOR AREA **970SQFT**
ARCHITECT/DESIGNER **FRANK CHIU/ONE: CHINA STUDIO**
PHOTOGRAPHER **VIRGILE SIMON BERTRAND**
TEXT **ANNA KOOR**

This apartment, situated in a quiet, leafy area of Mid-levels, has undergone an impressive renovation. Despite a modest, segregated floor space, a tight budget was one issue that deterred an indiscriminate demolition of internal walls. However, the cross wall that cut the flat in half was removed. Consequently, the living room gained the third bedroom, yielding more space, light and harbour views. Storage was the definitive must-have and several repositories that do not bulk-out into rooms have been orchestrated. A tatami-inspired sleeping surface that incorporates storage in the master bedroom is one example.

A new wall was constructed, which was to be the singular element for orienting events, objects and activities. With only one unit per floor, the apartment is fortunate to possess its own lobby, and this is where the wall begins, penetrating the front door and continuing in a straight line, unobstructed, until it hits the end elevation. The architect's methodology was to re-align the geometry of the flat to support a more sympathetic arrangement. Everything - kitchen, dining, sleeping quarters, bathroom, sofas, bookcase - lies perpendicular to the wall, thereby accentuating its presence. The effect is further heightened through the materials. The wall's smooth whiteness contrasts with the elements that are plugged into it, such as the metallic mesh door, the glass and steel of the dining and kitchen areas, and the natural timber bedroom platform.

Although the space was transformed, it retains the personality of its owners. The architect took this on board, even reflecting Bertrand's profession as a photographer in the design concept. The wall was treated like a frame outlining various "apertures" along the course of its route, the final shoot being a small vertical slot filled with translucent perspex, which allows light to filter into the bedroom from the sunny living space.

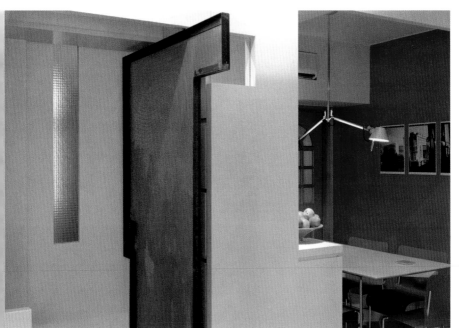

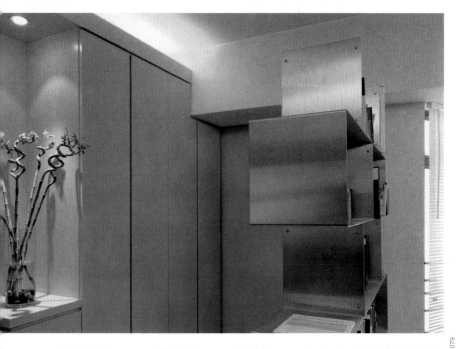

CONCEALED IN A CUBICLE

gary's apartment

With a compact and efficient layout of dual function space and concealed storage, this miniscule apartment manages to attain an attractive ambience for its occupant.

PROJECT LOCATION **ISLAND EAST, HONG KONG**
FLOOR AREA **330SQFT**
ARCHITECT/DESIGNER **EDGE (HK) LTD**
PHOTOGRAPHER **ALMOND CHU**
TEXT **ANNA KOOR**

The minute, 330 square foot apartment belongs to a bachelor and is tailor-made for his lifestyle and daily routine. Squeezing the normal functions of a fully working home into this amount of space was only possible by making spaces perform multiple roles. A compact and efficient arrangement of the kitchenette, bathroom and laundry area liberates the remaining space to fulfill the remaining necessities of bachelor life.

Surfaces are "dematerialised" and illumination is ambient, in order to give the appearance of a wider volume. The palette is dominated by white, translucent and transparent materials. However, as if in contrast, a full-height tower, built in solid cherry wood, intersects the space. This object accommodates the movie projector, refrigerator, washbasins and laundry machinery. Elsewhere, space is utilised through the multiple operations of partitions, lighting and mobile furniture. As with all homes, there is a need for storage to hide away the mundane accessories that support any lifestyle. Therefore, items such as books, CDs, clothing, pictures, stereo and videos are stacked on a chrome factory shelving system and hidden behind floating white curtains.

This leaves the central space free for the conduction of everyday rituals such as resting, working, dressing, reading, chatting, sleeping, and eating. The floor is washed with an unearthly glow of blue fluorescent light, whilst structural components are up-lit brightly to lend them articulation. The large front window is the apartment's aperture to the outside world, but when screened with a lowered blind it becomes a backdrop to the vastly different worlds of movies, news and the Internet projected from the tower.

A HARMONIC COMPOSITION

ken rose
apartment

Culinary and musical passions were the definitive influences on the design of this flexible apartment for a jazz musician.

PROJECT LOCATION **MID-LEVELS, HONG KONG**
FLOOR AREA **900SQFT**
ARCHITECT/DESIGNER **JASON CAROLINE DESIGN LTD/ARCHITUDE STUDIO**
PHOTOGRAPHER **ANDREW CHESTER ONG**
TEXT **ANNA KOOR**

The apartment is tucked away down in a low-rise cul-de-sac - a leafy
haven that is at odds with the surrounding gleaming modern residential
tower blocks. Its owner is a full-time professor and jazz musician. His
profession called for a number of stipulations in relation to the design.
The living room had to conform to certain dimensions for acoustic
perfection. Storage needed to take into consideration the client's vast
music collection. Finally, a practice room was required, preferably
private from the rest of the apartment, so as to cause minimal disturbance.

In plan, the interior radiates from a central core, creating a succession
of functional spaces that fold into one another via sliding and pivoting
doors. The architects' intention was to play with the dimensions and
the relationship between spaces. In one mode, the layout almost
resembles a conventional abode. However, in another, it becomes
completely open like a loft. Unusually, the heart of the space is the
bathroom, which dematerialises when frosted glass openings at its
ends are pushed back. It is almost a freestanding element, denoted
with raw concrete. Its permeability allows views through the apartment
and showcases the vanity washbasins. More importantly, during the
day, natural light filters through the space and at night, the opposite
occurs when the bathroom becomes a self-illuminated light box.

Culinary passions were a strong influence on the planning of the
kitchen. Its close proximity to the master bedroom would, under most
circumstances, be eschewed. However, in this case it was an
expressed desire. A raised glass floor accommodates recessed
lighting, which further lifts it up off the floor in a visual sense.
Underneath, the screed of the floor slab is left in its raw state and
relates to the raw concrete finish of the freestanding elements.

THE TRAVELLER'S HUB

paul hicks apartment

Work frequently takes Paul Hicks travelling around the region, which means time at home is all the more precious. The travel dimension has fed Hicks with some great ideas for the interior of his apartment.

PROJECT LOCATION **MID-LEVELS, HONG KONG**
FLOOR AREA **900SQFT**
ARCHITECT/DESIGNER **BHI LTD**
PHOTOGRAPHER **JOHN BUTLIN**
TEXT **ANNA KOOR**

Location was the chief factor while Hicks was searching for his new abode, primarily because he prefers for the different facets of his life (work, socialising, shopping) to be just a step away from his home. Another priority was that the apartment needed to be all things at all times: a place to catch up with work or catch up with sleep; a place to retreat and relax; and a place to entertain both formally and casually, for friends to drop by and hang out. With that in mind, Hicks was conscious of not overloading the apartment with clutter, so that the space would remain fluid and a sense of order would be maintained.

Designer Bruce Harwood has created an introverted space roughly divided into quadrants denoting the living room, bedroom, bathroom and kitchen. An unobtrusive wall-to-wall self-illuminating closet lines the back wall, which is home to all of Hicks' storage needs. An oversized bath is custom-built into the corner and wrapped in black mosaic tiles. It is enclosed by frosted glass, which forms a glowing box at night. In the kitchen/dining/living zones, there is a gradation of the colour palette, from steel and darker timbers to neutrals and whites, respectively. Many of the soft furnishings and accessories were sourced in Thailand, adding a sense of Asian flair to what is otherwise a very monochromatic background. The open kitchen maintains visual uniformity despite being "patchworked" from custom-designed and proprietary furniture.

A backlit glass half-wall forms a glowing interface between the bedroom and living room, enabling the owner to watch movies whilst in bed. A raised floor plinth of bleached white timber designates the bedroom zone, creating a more intimate finish than the concrete that covers the remaining floor. The difference in level creates a psychological barrier - when there is a crowd in the apartment, it tends to discourage guests from roaming too far.

HIDING AWAY

peak apartment

Living the life of a minimalist is often easier said than done, particularly for a family. The drive towards minimalism was enabled in this apartment, only by considering every possible function in order to then tuck away as many extraneous items as possible.

PROJECT LOCATION **THE PEAK, HONG KONG**
ARCHITECT/DESIGNER **KPLUSK ASSOCIATES**
PHOTOGRAPHER **GRAHAM UDEN**
TEXT **ANNA KOOR**

The pursuit of perfection through simplifying form and material has to be poised against practical realities. The owners had every intention of achieving the former. As is typical of KplusK's interior endeavours, every non-structural element in the apartment was erased, freeing them to design from a blank canvas. The envelope is extruded into several pockets, which presented the opportunity to tuck away non-central functions - such as the scullery, maid's suite, and storage - into minor zones and be left with a cleaner plan. With spectacular views of ocean and lush forest flanking both long elevations, the mean-windowed facades were punched out and enlarged into single glazed openings.

A polar ash floor provides a flesh-coloured surface from which to anchor several key architectural components. The main entertaining zone is intersected by a chimney breast which was re-rendered in cement and fitted with a remote-controlled electric flame fire. This provides a convenient node from which to orientate the kitchen, dining, living and sleeping areas. In the kitchen, a long centrepiece workbench is a medium for simultaneous cooking and conversation, a meeting point between family members and friends. Messy operations such as cleaning dishes, chopping and preparation are pulled out of sight to a support kitchen at the rear.

The master bedroom has unusually close proximity to the kitchen and family activities, but can revert to a private sanctuary when required. Views are filtered by a sliding wall of frosted glass panels. When opened, it reveals an intermediate zone - the en suite bathroom - the focus of which is a freestanding vanity unit and washbasin constructed from Shanghainese sandblasted slate. On its reverse, the component serves as the headboard to the bed. A pair of doors hung on either side of the vanity wall enables the bedroom to be closed off completely, and when open, the doors recess fully into the walls. Throughout the apartment, devices are created to hide extraneous equipment, light switches, surround-sound speakers, computers, blinds, and so on.

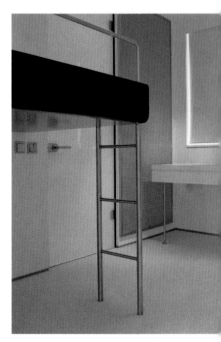

A TEMPORARY OASIS

shama apartment 1

In the luxury serviced apartment bracket, temporary homes flushed with all the accessories of the most stylish of hotels are fast becoming the new way of living in Asia. Shama stems from an ancient Sanskrit word meaning "tranquility, restfulness, an oasis of calm" and this sums up what the developer and their designer aimed to deliver to their residents.

PROJECT LOCATION **CAUSEWAY BAY, HONG KONG**
FLOOR AREA **1170SQFT**
ARCHITECT/DESIGNER **DILLON GARRIS**
PHOTOGRAPHER **KELLEY CHENG**
TEXT **ANNA KOOR**

This generously sized apartment was created for the mobile executive who wants all the comforts of home whilst travelling on business, minus the fuss of a five-star hotel, but with all the luxuries. It was apparent that Shama's guests would also require the additional amenities one expects from a private apartment, such as a kitchen. Most importantly, there was the need to emphasise the unique and personal, rather than the anonymity, of a cloned hotel room. There was the need to provide a balance between business and personal life whilst celebrating Hong Kong's vibrant lifestyle.

The mood of this apartment is contemporary and stylish, with a distinctly Asian feel. Having previously worked with Christian Liagre, Paris-based Garris is skilled in the art of quality finishes and precisely crafted timbers. Personalisation is enhanced by Garris' custom-designed furniture in solid maple or walnut. Furthermore, he was not afraid to seek out the atypical in terms of soft furnishings. A goatskin daybed rubs shoulders with a solid maple chair and a silk floor lamp. The floors are honed from solid long planks of Argentine brown Incensio wood.

Another parameter to the brief was the need to be international in appeal, while exuding a definite Asian charm. Attention to this detail was overseen directly by the Shama team, who regularly travel the world to source soft furnishings, textiles, ceramics, linen, original artwork and floor coverings. However, the attitude is modern Asian rather than anything ethnic. Often, the only clue might be in colour - a ripe aubergine, a vibrant red, or simply the more earthy tones that are akin to Japanese interiors. The accessories include Thai silk, glazed Celadon-ware, cashmere, Nepalese rugs and Spanish leather. Original artwork by emerging Chinese artists complete the picture.

NO COMPROMISES

shama apartment 2

The planning of this living space positively challenges the assumption that small is by nature cramped and awkward. While spaces take on multiple uses, the comfort of this boutique living environment is maximised.

PROJECT LOCATION **CAUSEWAY BAY, HONG KONG**
FLOOR AREA **730SQFT**
ARCHITECT/DESIGNER **DILLON GARRIS**
PHOTOGRAPHER **KELLEY CHENG**
TEXT **ANNA KOOR**

This bijou home is only inches away from the frenetic shopping and entertainment hubbub of Causeway Bay, which is what makes it so attractive as an immediate retreat right at the doorstep. The Paris-based designer was commissioned to visualise a boutique living environment where style and individuality are given equal weight to comfort and functionality.

Luxury is not compromised by the fairly modest 730 square foot dimensions of this one-bedroom unit. In fact the planning of this living space positively challenges the assumption that small is by nature cramped and awkward. There were significant concerns such as the availability of only one window. Lack of light is mitigated by the use of single-ply Thai silk screens, which divide the bed from the living quarters. The designer did not hold back on other essentials, such as the closet space (which is disproportionately generous), a king-size bed with sumptuous linen, and an openly streamlined bathroom.

Multi-purpose usage enables the occupant to achieve maximum usage of the space. The dining table doubles as a work desk, the ceramic stools couple as side tables, and the chaise longue sofa becomes a guest bed. Folding back the timber wall panels in the hallway reveals a small kitchen containing all the vital necessities. In the bathroom, this strategy is also evident with the mirror, which doubles as a light and storage cupboard. The layering of different functions has been designed as a series of smooth transitions in this apartment.

CURIOSITY CABINET

wong apartment

Sunaqua Concepts has made the most of a small space to provide a comfortable home centred around a collection of books and electronic toys.

PROJECT LOCATION **TSING YI, HONG KONG**
FLOOR AREA **475SQFT**
ARCHITECT/DESIGNER **SUNAQUA CONCEPTS LTD**
PHOTOGRAPHER **DICK**
TEXT **ANNA KOOR**

Overlooking the hulking industrial-scape of Tsing Yi's shipping container terminals, this flat at Villa Esplanada, is by contrast, diminutive in form. The young, newly married couple who own the apartment embarked on a renovation programme with a very tight budget. The floor plan is typically cramped. Without demolishing any walls, except for a minor partition between the hallway and dining area, the designer manages to open up the apartment in other ways.

Sun Wong from Sunaqua Concepts began the design process by examining his clients' focus of enjoyment - in this case, a vast collection of books and electronic toys. The intention was to project the character of the owners and promote comfort and intimacy with their surroundings. Therefore the first objective was to devise a storage and display system suitable for their collections. This is designed as a continuous frame that lines the walls and ceiling between the dining and living areas. The composite structure of raw steel supports a series of suspended open oak timber crates or trays.

With space being severely limited, Wong played down the features of the envelope to smooth out the surfaces. Air conditioning units are concealed behind louvres. The straw lines of the wallpaper help to maintain the continuity, and intervening doors and closets are also disguised behind its wrapping. A minimal use of material and colour also serves to expand the space visually. The kitchen door was changed from solid hinged to sliding glass, which is partially acid-etched and mirrored, creating an illusory slot of space. In the study and guestroom, a fold-down bed is recessed into the built-in furniture and the windowsill is utilised as a prop for a custom-built oak workstation. A constricting entrance to the master bedroom is dematerialised with mirror, also creating a dressing area. The windowsill is again appropriated as an extension to the bed.

MINIMUM RESIDENCE

9 tubo house

The functionality and beauty of a 50-year-old model for space-making is resurrected in this "minimum residence".

PROJECT LOCATION **MITAKA, TOKYO**
ARCHITECT/DESIGNER **MAKOTO KOIZUMI**
PHOTOGRAPHER **SOICHI MURAZUMI**
TEXT **REIKO KASAI**

"Tubo" is the traditional unit of measurement in Japan. 1 tubo is roughly equivalent to 3.3 square metres.

9 Tubo House is the house that interior designer Akoto Koizumi remade based on the original 1957 structure designed by the late architect Makoto Masuzawa. The original house was known for its small but extremely comfortable space. For a 1999 exhibition, a structural model of the "minimum residence" was reproduced. The curator, Shu Hagiwara, approached Koizumi to redesign and convert his own mansion based upon this same concept. Many people were attracted to its functionality and beauty, and started requesting for the same design. Producer Ysuyuki Okazaki commercialised the "9 Tubo House" design, and has since created what is nearly an industry based on it.

Okazaki proposed five principles for the creation of a "residence with minimal space". The first of these is to establish a square plane of 3 ma x 3 ma (3 ma is about 5.5 metres). The next is to insert a stairwell of 3 tubo (9.9 metres). Externally, the gable should be 3 metres by 3 metres with an eave height of 14.8 feet (about 4.5 metres). Also, there should be a round pillar in the house. Finally, the main façade should have a width of 12 feet (about 3.7 metres) and a height of 13 feet (about 4 metres). He explains, "These five principles are like the OS of the computer, each designer should develop applications that run on it."

A BURROWING BUILDING

beaver house

On a tiny site with soft ground, the designers of this house have both burrowed underground and reached for the sky.

PROJECT LOCATION **KOTO-KU, TOKYO**
ARCHITECT/DESIGNER **AKIRA YONEDA AND MASAHIRO IKEDA**
PHOTOGRAPHER **KOJI OKUMURA**
TEXT **REIKO KASAI**

This is a small residence on a site near the Ara River, which architect, Akira Yoneda, and structural designer, Masahiro Ikeda, have designed together. A high artificial riverbank obstructs a direct view to the river from nearby locations. For this reason, the client requested that the house be constructed as high up as possible, so that views could be afforded from the upper floors. Due to the soft soil conditions of the site, this request could not be entirely fulfilled. Thus, the designers extended the building to the maximum limit of the site. The structure is buried half-underground, forming what is like a floating ship on soft ground.

The first floor, containing the living and dining rooms, is below ground level. Although there are no windows, plenty of natural light filters through skylights that are mounted along the ceiling edge. An open, cantilevered staircase rises delicately upward, and leads to the master bedroom, which is projected outwards as if floating from the building. A spiral staircase leads further up to a child's room. The roof, which can be reached from the balcony on the topmost level, offers a breathtaking view of the river.

The interior is sleek and uncluttered, composed with a base palette of white finishes, and punctuated by black coloured elements such as architectonic planes of shelving and window frames. The double-height ceiling of the living room also appears to extend the perception that this narrow space is seemingly spacious.

SCENES AND SPECTACLES

borzoi house

This courtyard house, of a somewhat futuristic appearance, contains various scenes and spectacles within its surrounding walls, and an unsuspected openness.

PROJECT LOCATION **CHIBA PREFECTURE, JAPAN**
FLOOR AREA **933SQFT**
ARCHITECT/DESIGNER **NORISADA MAEDA/N MAEDA ATELIER**
PHOTOGRAPHER **HIROSHI SHINOZAWA**
TEXT **KWAH MENG CHING**

Sitting on a site of over 3,200 square feet, this courtyard house is unique and eye-catching. The most striking point about this house is undoubtedly its form. Lying on a low plinth is a form of an elongated elliptical cross section, with a radius of curvature that is different at both ends. The metallic exterior skin, which shines and glistens under the sun, further renders the house a futuristic quality that distinguishes it from its neighbours.

Yet, this seemingly closed form, with no apparent windows to the exterior, speaks a different story once its exterior wall is penetrated. The entrance foyer is in a courtyard garden. A curved wall on one side sets the tone for the remaining parts of the house. The whitewashed interior spaces, along with the three internal courtyard gardens, give the inward-looking house an openness that is otherwise unsuspected when one is outside.

To designer Maeda, a courtyard is a powerful architectural element that can generate various scenes and spectacles with its surrounding walls. Aiming to create a relationship between "one" and "many" – i.e. one exterior form and many interior scenes – he united the three courtyards with one seamless plane that surfaces from the turf. Within this form, he wanted to further make the various scenes that occur within this house mix and fuse together. What results is a simple house, where the lives within perform and revolve around the courtyards, depending on it for views to the sky, and also penetration of light and fresh air. The external form of the house is unique, but the living spaces of the inhabitants are in no way compromised by it. Instead, the departure from the usual straight lines of a house have enriched the living atmosphere and expanded on the interpretation of a typical courtyard house.

SHARE AND SHARE ALIKE

c house

This house on a small site has two floors of commercial restaurant space wrapping around a private living core in the configuration of a letter C. The distinct boundary between public and private is diluted, transgressed and shared.

PROJECT LOCATION **TOKYO, JAPAN**
FLOOR AREA **1227SQFT**
ARCHITECT/DESIGNER **TOSHIMITSU KUNO, NOBUYUKI NOMURA, TELE-DESIGN COLLABORATIVE NETWORK**
PHOTOGRAPHER **TATSUYA NOAKI**
TEXT **KWAH MENG CHING**

Located at the junction where five roads intersect, C House is different from the countless other "faceless" buildings in the surrounding urban fabric. This difference is manifested in both the architectural treatment of the volume, as well as the functional programme of the project.

Built on a site area of a mere 646 square feet, the building has a footprint of 452 square feet. Its floor area is spread over two basements and two storeys. The structure – part steel frame, part reinforced concrete - is being used as both a private residence and a restaurant. While such mixed-usage programmes are not uncommon in traditional shophouses around Asia, there is a slightly different interpretation in the C House. In traditional shophouses, there is a clear stratification of functions, with the commercial programmes conventionally located on the ground level, and the residences above. However, C House boasts a different scheme of organisation, with the self-contained private flat being in the middle, while the commercial programmes are arranged both above and below the private housing. This redefinition of the public/private relationship in an urban living environment attempts to steer away from the distinct duality of public and private, moving instead towards a more encompassing configuration, whereby the public commercial space is "wrapped" around the private residence. The distinct boundary between public and private is thus diluted, transgressed and shared here.

Architecturally, the residence forms an enclosed box "floating" between the glassed commercial spaces. Both the residence and the commercial spaces enjoy their own respective access points. The commercial space on the second storey is accessed by the lower basement, while a separate entrance to the residence leads one directly into the commercial spaces, further bridging the two contrasting spheres of activity within this unconventional design.

FIGURE AND GROUND

hachijo atelier

The Hachijo Atelier is an inquiry into the concept of "architecture as landscape", based on the relatedness between the architectural "figure" and the diverse surrounding "ground" of the natural environment.

PROJECT LOCATION **HACHIJO ISLAND, TOKYO, JAPAN**
ARCHITECT/DESIGNER **NORIHIKO DAN/NORIHIKO DAN AND ASSOCIATES**
PHOTOGRAPHER **MITSUMASA FUJITSUKA**
TEXT **KWAH MENG CHING**

Norihiko Dan is interested in the concept of the liquidity of "ground" and the amalgamation of architectural volume with soil. This house marks an early attempt in his exploration of this new relationship made between manmade forms and the natural environment. The idea is later manifested in larger-scale projects like the Hiyoshi Dam and the swimming pool complex in Kyoto.

Surrounded by a verdant tropical landscape, the Hachijo Atelier sits on a westward-facing slope overlooking picturesque black cliffs by the Pacific Ocean. This is a vacation home and studio for the architect's father - who is a composer and author - with an exterior performance space for Taiko drumming.

The dual role of the house, being a private retreat as well as an open-air theatre at the same time, necessitates a careful balance between architectural enclosure and openness. The private spaces of the home are organised compactly into a fortress-like volume with a bow-shaped plan; the two bedrooms, atelier and the wet areas are arranged on the "bowstring" side, with fenestrations opening to the views. The living room opens up towards the south and is fronted by the outdoor terrace. In fact, the outdoor terraces can be said to be as much a part of the "interior" of the house as the rest of the spaces are - the only difference being that they are open to the sky. These flagstone-paved terraces fan out to the south and provide a natural extension to the interior living spaces. Together with the stage located at the end of the site, they form a big open-air theatre with public seating areas for when performances are held. The roof terrace on top of the house resembles the deck of a ship, overlooking the surroundings and the performing area.

NATURALLY COOLED

house at matsubara

A careful composition of folding planes and fenestrations have created a house that can be naturally cooled with breezes, without the requirement of air-conditioning.

PROJECT LOCATION **SETAGAYA-KU, JAPAN**
ARCHITECT/DESIGNER **SATOSHI OKADA**
PHOTOGRAPHER **HIROYUKI HIRAI**
TEXT **REIKO KASAI & TATSUO ISO**

This sparsely filled, rectangular shaped residence emphasises volumes and planes. It has two skins that wrap and fold to carve out exterior courtyards and the interior spaces of the home. Concrete walls set at a height of 5.8 metres enclose the house. The perimeter wall is constructed in lightweight reinforced concrete, while unit slabs of a lightweight steel frame structure are used for the roof. The living and dining rooms, as well as a kitchen, are located on the first floor, whereas the bedroom, tearoom, bathroom and toilet are located on the ground floor.

The courtyard on the western front is a large area that receives much sunlight, such that temperatures are easily elevated. On the other hand, the courtyard at the eastern rear is more sheltered, so it is not easily warmed. When openings on both the eastern and western sides are opened, air flows naturally through the house. The skylight at the top of the stair volume is also effective for cross-ventilation. The cool air of the ground floor area flows up to replace the warm air that escapes from upstairs. Since concrete walls have high heat-retaining capacities, heat dissipation does not stop even after sunset. Hence, this circulation of air continues till night. A comfortable indoor environment is thus achieved without the use of air-conditioning.

Aside from the comforting flow of breeze, the significant openings in this house establish interesting vistas and lines of sight. Skylights and views to the courtyards provide restful outlooks within a succinct and rather horizontal space. The verticality of the open stair volume also provides a captivating spatial play.

A SHADOW IN THE FOREST

house at mount fuji

An appreciation and consideration of a stunning natural landscape have shaped this theatrical house on the foothills of Mount Fuji, which sits in perfect harmony with its surroundings.

PROJECT LOCATION **YAMANASHI PREFECTURE, JAPAN**
ARCHITECT/DESIGNER **SATOSHI OKADA/SATOSHI OKADA ARCHITECTS**
PHOTOGRAPHER **HIROYUKI HIRAI**
TEXT **KWAH MENG CHING**

Situated 1,200 metres above sea-level amongst a tree plantation on the northern foothills of Mount Fuji is this weekend villa. On the gently inclined site are a number of deciduous trees and there is a forest of white birch towards the north. The client wanted to build a small house here to appreciate the tranquility of the surrounding nature; to capitalise on the pleasant views filled with sunlight, trees and undulating landscape.

A diagonally folded wall divides the house volume into two realms – one is a big living space and the other contains the bedrooms and a bathroom. The ceiling height in the living room gradually changes from 3.8 metres to 5.3 metres in accordance with the sloping roof. To contrast with the generous space here, the dining and kitchen are compressed beneath the loft as a space with a 2-metre-high ceiling. The progression through the house is spatially dramatic, and induces an appreciation of the natural surroundings. When one first enters the house, the entrance area is dark enough for one to appreciate the skylight down the hall at the living area. As one proceeds towards the living, the tall, narrow and dim space gradually becomes taller, broader and brighter along the folded wall. The afternoon sunlight pierces theatrically through a small skylight and washes the white wall that lies opposite.

Okada has shown extreme control when dealing with this site so that even fabricated, unnatural additions sit in perfect harmony with the beautiful landscape. When viewed from the exterior, the sloping roof is cleverly pitched according to the gradient of the terrain. The use of black stained Japanese cedar for the outer wall cladding further pays homage to the site. Between rustling leaves above and turf below, the villa stands like an upheaval of the land, where the black lava has slept since ancient times. Like a dark band in between the green, it exists in harmony with nature, like "a shadow in the forest".

FUTURISTIC AND FLEXIBLE

k house lounge

Despite a small floor area, the renovation of the second storey of this house for a two-generation household demonstrates an understanding of the contemporary urban environment. It proposes a space for a new independent urban lifestyle.

PROJECT LOCATION **CENTRAL TOKYO, JAPAN**
FLOOR AREA **484SQFT**
ARCHITECT/DESIGNER **HIROYUKI MATSUSHIMA/D.M.A.**
PHOTOGRAPHER **D.M.A.**
TEXT **KWAH MENG CHING**

For Hiroyuki Matsushima of DMA, it has become increasingly difficult to create a dwelling space within the contemporary urban environment by relying on former architectural ideologies. This is so because the rituals of dining and living, which have traditionally been performed within the house, are now being carried out more regularly in the urban landscape. The city, with its extensive network of restaurants, cafes and convenience stores, is like the kitchen, living and dining rooms for the urban dweller. Matsushima feels that since domestic functions have infiltrated the urbanscape, the physical living and dining rooms of a house should not be a closed internal environment. Instead, they should open out, extend to and connect with the urban expanse.

The client requested for a new home environment that corresponds with the changes of an urban lifestyle. DMA responded by inserting a neutral furniture-like tube into the existing house. It has transformed the once stagnant space into one that allows more flexible activity. Seeking inspiration from Issey Miyake's A-POC stretch-knit fabric, DMA's tube creates a condition where the floor, wall and ceiling are united and flexibility is afforded through the structural framework. For example, by cutting the tube at a certain place, it can be widened to create an opening for an entrance. With one more cut, the section becomes a sliding door. Cutting in slits creates louvres that allow the possibilities of controlling views, sound and the passage of light.

DMA has designed the living room of this urban residence like a satellite space of urban life. It is flexible and allows for changes of scene in the floor-oriented residential lifestyle. For example, it can become a lounge for unwinding, a workspace to sit down with the laptop, or even a place for slumber with the provision of a simple bed.

INTO THE VOID

m house

A long and narrow living area is made spacious and airy by a triple-height internal void space in this light-filled house.

PROJECT LOCATION **SETAGAYA-KU, TOKYO**
ARCHITECT/DESIGNER **EISHIN MATSUNAGA@CLIP**
PHOTOGRAPHER **CLIP**
TEXT **REIKO KASAI & TATSUO ISO**

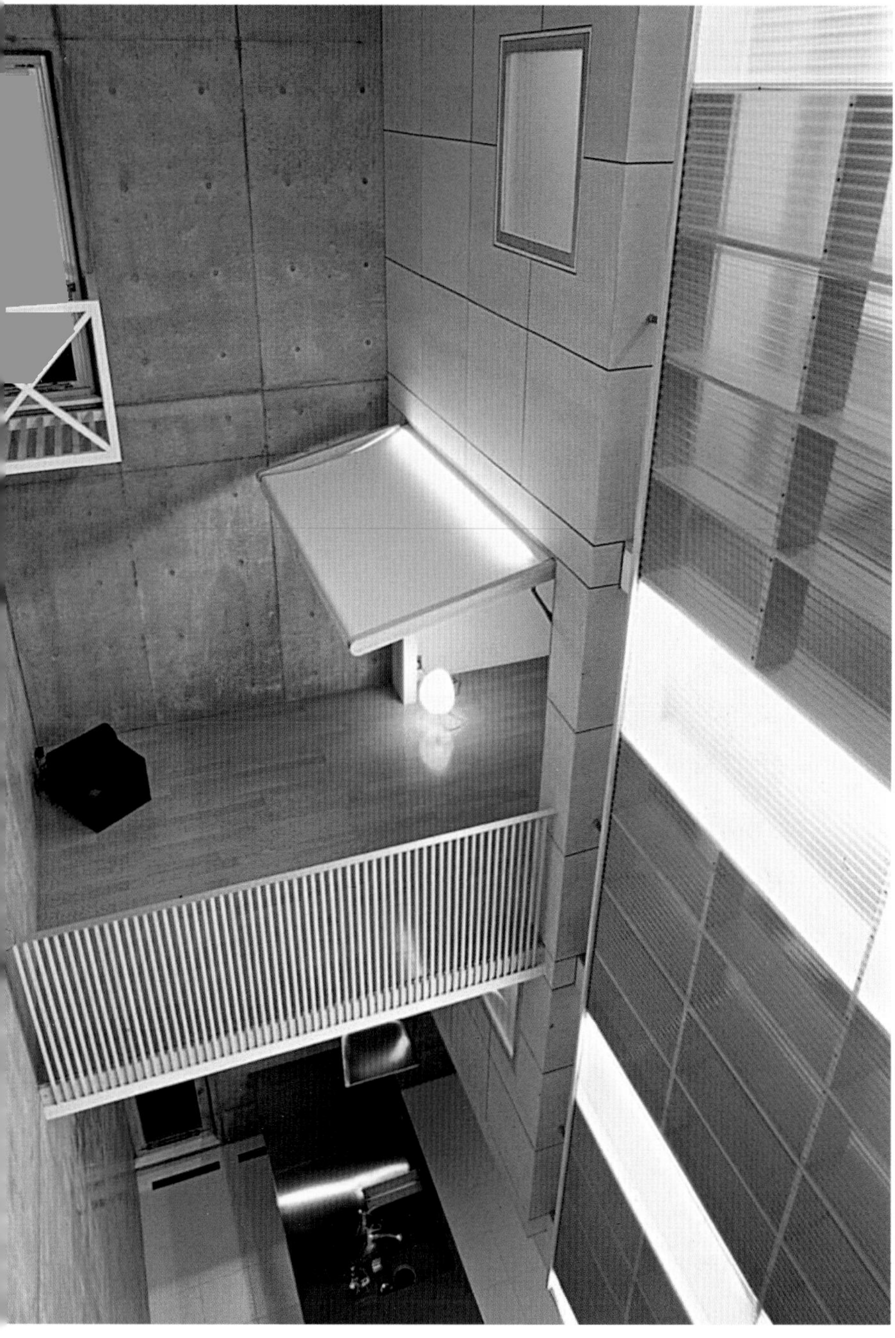

The M House is located in a densely packed residential neighbourhood in Tokyo. Its height is about 9 metres, and it contains 3 floors configured about a triple height internal void. The house is divided into two zones: a formal (or public) western zone, incorporating the triple height void, and an informal (or private) eastern zone, enclosing the bedroom, stairs and storage area. In addition, there is a single "room" on each of the upper floors that protrudes into the void space. These function as work/study and sitting spaces, and have a verandah-like configuration overlooking the living and dining areas below on the ground floor. The bathroom is on the third floor.

The living area is very long and narrow, but the internal height and light make it feel generously spacious. One long wall is finished in polished concrete, which shimmers with the light that filters inside through the large windows at each short end of the space. The other long side wall is covered by shelving that is backed with a translucent material, allowing a filtration of light between the public and private zones. The house enjoys natural light in each room by having a big top-light and large windows.

A roller screen is installed between the two zones. It is moveable and can be extended into the formal zone space. Residents can see through the stairwell onto the other side. This stairwell space functions as a 3-dimensional courtyard. It helps to maintain a warm indoor temperature. The warmed air, which collects on the upper part of stairwell, is discharged in summer, and insulates the house during winter.

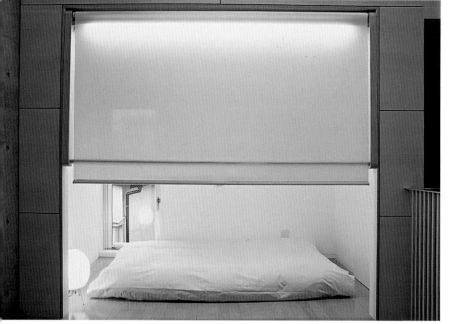

A GEM OF LIGHT

natural illuminance

This house, for a young couple, is like a little gem that distinguishes itself from the surrounding conventional abodes. It may be small and inward-looking, but its white box is filled with light and air that enriches the soul.

PROJECT LOCATION **TOKYO, JAPAN**
FLOOR AREA **715SQFT**
ARCHITECT/DESIGNER **MASAKI ENDOH + MASAHIRO IKEDA (EDH ENDOH DESIGN HOUSE + MIAS)**
PHOTOGRAPHER **MASAKI ENDOH**
TEXT **KWAH MENG CHING**

The clients had requested for a house where they could be surrounded by light in their daily life and yet be oblivious to the prying eyes of surrounding neighbours. A simple request it may seem to be, but the difficulty here is that the house is located in highly built-up Tokyo. However, architect Masaki Endoh and engineer Masahiro Ikeda have splendidly negotiated this situation and created an eye-catching house with charming spaces within.

This cubic building has a symmetrically composed wrap-around facade of white square panels, with slit glass separating each of them. The architect has adopted this treatment in anticipation of future houses being built on a field to the south of the site. Being in a northern temperate climate, the sun rises from the east and predominantly hovers in the south, before setting in the west. The white wrap-around facade has maximised this sun path and floods the interior with a brightness that is soothing, but not glaring. It also shields the house from the eyes of the neighbours. With its lights switched on at night, the house looks like a big lantern or like a giant spaceship that has just landed from outer space.

The northern facade of the house has a different treatment, with two structural columns painted black. The wet areas are concentrated in one area and finished with glass as far as possible to give an illusion of the expansion of space. The main space within the house is the living-cum-dining room, which occupies nearly one-third of the total house area. With a ceiling height of 4 metres, this space allows for the possible future addition of a loft. Being in this space held behind the white-panelled wall, one is constantly embraced by spirit-lifting soft light that filters through the slit glass. Some of the white panels can be further opened to allow for cross-ventilation of air.

AWAITING DISCOVERY

oh house

This house for a family of three, tucked away from the scrutiny of the public on an L-shaped site, uses minimum means to achieve maximum effect.

PROJECT LOCATION **CHIBA PREFECTURE, JAPAN**
FLOOR AREA **699SQFT**
ARCHITECT/DESIGNER **AKO NAGAO/AKO NAGAO ARCHITECT OFFICE**
PHOTOGRAPHER **SATOSHI ASAKAWA**
TEXT **KWAH MENG CHING**

Hidden from public view, this house does not face the usual problem of maintaining privacy within a public setting. Instead, the critical issue here lies in creating a house that can be opened to the exterior. What has resulted is a 1-storey rectangular volume that capitalises on the longitudinal orientation of the site, creating a spacious garden on the southern front. The elevated floor of the house further renders the illusion that it is floating over the garden.

Internally, the layout of the house resembles that of a one-room apartment. The main storage area and wet areas are all organised at one end near the entrance. Passing through this walled enclosure within the box, one arrives at the main space of the house. The living, dining and sleeping areas are all organised compactly into one "partitionless" space. The folding doors on both sides of this space can be opened to the garden. Psychologically, the space is extended beyond the confines of the built form. Environmentally, the open concept of the house allows for good cross-ventilation and eliminates the need for air-conditioning for most of the year.

The rectangular volume is further articulated with protruding eaves on its longitudinal elevations. This simple gesture not only gives the mundane rectilinear form a much-needed difference; in a functional sense, it also helps to shade the interior spaces from the scorching sun during summer. On the whole, the house does not try to be loud or attention seeking. It is simple but thoughtful in its execution, whilst shaping an extremely liveable environment.

RADICAL FORM-MAKING

rooftecture m

Expanding on his earlier architectural explorations, Shuhei Endo has created a home where the family can live together as a whole, in a continuous strip of partially shared living space that produces various relationships.

PROJECT LOCATION FUKUI PREFECTURE, JAPAN
ARCHITECT/DESIGNER SHUHEI ENDO/SHUHEI ENDO ARCHITECT INSTITUTE
PHOTOGRAPHER YOSHIHARU MATSUMURA
TEXT KWAH MENG CHING

Rooftecture M is a house-cum-atelier. Located in a flat residential area 3 hours by train from Osaka, the rectangular site has a small frontage with elongated sides. The client had requested the inclusion of an atelier where he could receive visitors, with the more private family spaces being as inconspicuous to the visitors as possible. Shuhei Endo proposed a solution whereby the different functional spaces are sheltered under a huge piece of bent corrugated metal sheet, acting as both the roof and walls along both long sides. This piece of metal is cut at a few locations to admit air and light.

In terms of spatial organisation, the wet areas are tightly arranged into a rectangular volume on the ground floor at the centre, separating the entrance and car porch on both sides. The communal dining and living spaces are positioned towards the rear, so that activities within these spaces will not be visible to visitors as they make their way to the atelier. Located upstairs are the atelier and bedrooms.

Shuhei Endo's works are characterised by his continuous experiments in expanding the possibilities of modern architecture. In many instances, he tries to combine both the roof and walls as a single continuous member. By so doing, he reduces the architectural space into one continuous flowing volume. This approach proved to be very successful in his award-winning Springtecture H scheme, whereby functions are organised within a continuous curling strip of corrugated steel sheet. Here, in Rooftecture M, he develops this language further and demonstrates that such a form-making concept can be further extended to spaces of a larger area to work functionally as well.

DELICATE FILTRATIONS

screen house at senkawa

The problems of a tiny floor area and some specific client demands have been transformed into an attractive and ingenious architectural solution using a timber screen.

PROJECT LOCATION **TOSHIMA-KU, TOKYO**
FLOOR AREA **1291SQFT**
ARCHITECT/DESIGNER **MIKIO TAI/ARCHITECT CAFÉ**
PHOTOGRAPHER **KATSUHISA KIDA**
TEXT **REIKO KASAI & TATSUO ISO**

This house has an extremely small footprint, measuring only 430 square feet. The architect thus had to devise some clever strategies for planning in a tight space. On top of this, the client had also set certain demands of the space: that ventilation should be excellent; that there should be a sliding shutter for security; and that there should be the ability to sleep with the windows open in summer. These demands have in fact helped the architect to arrive at an inventive solution.

As the spatial area is very limited, using the indoor area for the stairs would not have been efficient. Instead, they are installed outside the main building envelope in a half-external space, enclosed by a screen that can be opened and closed. The screen has a wooden crease door that is slit to regulate the amount of sunlight, ventilation and privacy. The owners can change the open-and-closed state and position of the screen freely according to their preferences. This device is very effective for both environment regulation and crime prevention. For a young couple planning to expand their limited existing living space, this has proved to be a very good solution.

The top floor space is covered by lumber of two sizes, stacked against one another. This creates an interesting ribbed ceiling, which successfully brings the aesthetic of the external screen into the interior. The screen creates an attractive and delicate filtration of light both during the day and night.

SCULPTING FROM HISTORY

studio yukobo

A charming ex-clinic building, built by the client's grandfather, has been converted to a gallery for visiting artists and connected to an existing house in this renovation and conversion project.

PROJECT LOCATION TOKYO, JAPAN
ARCHITECT/DESIGNER TOMOAKI TANAKA/FORMS
PHOTOGRAPHER FORMS
TEXT KWAH MENG CHING

This project involves addition and alteration work to a house owned by a husband (who is a retired businessman) and wife (who is a sculptor). The couple has started an organisation to support young artists, inviting them to stay at their residence and create work. Not only did they need additional studio and gallery space, but they were also in need of improved accommodation for themselves. Hence, the project ultimately involved three aspects of work: the addition to their existing wooden house, the transformation of a neighbouring 50-year-old clinic building into a gallery space, and the insertion of a studio space in which a sculptor would work. In response to such a brief, Tomoaki Tanaka of FORMS opted to reorganise and optimise the existing building resources, instead of demolishing all and rebuilding.

The clinic building is a charming historical creation with a riveted truss structure. The designer chose to retain it to conserve the lost building technology, as well as to forge a connection between the past and the future. All the partitions and drop-ceilings were removed to reveal the aged structural elements, steel trusses and pre-cast concrete. Interventions are kept to a minimum with only the necessary partitions and equipment installed to facilitate the hosting of exhibitions in this space. On the other hand, a new volume with a pitched roof was added to the wooden house to create a second storey. This volume houses residential facilities and substitutes the rooms on the ground floor, which have been turned into a residence for visiting artists.

A new steel structure has been inserted between the wooden structure and the old clinic building. Functioning as a studio space, this structure is placed at an intersection such that its facade is designed as a response to the streetscape. The composition of the large sliding doors, steel frame, horizontal glass and spiral staircase unite the existing and new elements into a cohesive whole. This project is truly a sensitive restoration that respects the old, while the new insertion speaks a language of its time.

SYMBIOTIC SANCTUARY

t-set

The symbiotic dependency of two houses on one plot of land has enabled them to enjoy what other houses in the area may not enjoy: views, light and privacy.

PROJECT LOCATION **TOKYO, JAPAN**
FLOOR AREA **614SQFT**
ARCHITECT/DESIGNER **MANABU CHIBA/CHIBA MANABU ARCHITECTS**
PHOTOGRAPHER **NACASA & PARTNERS INC**
TEXT **KWAH MENG CHING**

Manabu Chiba designs houses in a way similar to how he would design a cityscape. Instead of creating enclosed and inward-looking houses, his houses afford a great degree of porosity that engages the occupants with the cityscape, whilst not compromising privacy and comfort. T-set is a further development of his ideas and an attempt at urban design and planning, albeit on a small scale.

T-set is actually the second of a pair of houses located in a residential area of Tokyo. The client bought a plot of land large enough to develop two independent detached houses. However, after close examination, Chiba found that to adopt the conventional site planning approach of dividing the land equally in the longitudinal direction would not work here. The houses would have become long, narrow and too contrived for comfortable living. Hence, Chiba sub-divided the land into one L-plot and another rectangular plot. Together, the two plots of land form a "T". The T-set house sits on the L-shaped plot. Both plots have their respective car-parking space, and both provide a view out to the neighbourhood. They also enjoy the presence of light and most important of all, a certain degree of privacy.

Houses in Tokyo are generally typified by their small size and close proximity to their neighbours, so much so that sometimes views, light and privacy are greatly compromised. Without exception, T-set is small and compact. Yet, with some lateral thinking and a refusal to accept the norm, the architect has provided the grounds for exploration of the constraints. Once inside the house, the high ceiling and the presence of a view out has helped to expand the small space psychologically. Its high degree of porosity and engagement with the cityscape have provided a different lesson on living in the city.

CONTEMPPORARY ASIAN

damansara
perdana

Custom-made furniture and Asian art adorn neutral surfaces in this apartment show unit.

PROJECT LOCATION **BANDAR DAMANSARA, MALAYSIA**
ARCHITECT/DESIGNER **SUSANNE ZEIDLER, NG KIEN TECK/ZLG SDN BHD**
PHOTOGRAPHER **K.L. NG**
TEXT **RICHARD SE**

The concept for this show unit was to use a contemporary approach with "Asian" accents and highlights. The background palette of the space is neutral, but finishes and decorative items display a distinct 'Asianess'. Many of the display items selected by the client and the designers have been created by Asian artists, and were specifically chosen for this reason. They are composed and displayed throughout the show unit wherever suitable. The colour scheme is primarily composed of different hues of purple contrasting with different hues of grey. This was of great importance to the selection process of all the cushions, curtains, roman blinds, furniture and even the display items, which have all been selected to complement one another.

Wall elevations are treated like compositions of shapes and colours. Antique tapestries are hung on the walls, either framed in gold or suspended between two pieces of perspex. In the dining area, a cantilevered wall cabinet hangs in composition with a set of images by a Malaysian artist, framed in stainless steel, above it. Display niches in the hallway display more art. Most of the loose furniture was custom-made. The main material used is local timber veneer, finished either in a lime wash or a dark varnish. Often these two main surface finishes appear directly next to each other in the furniture designs, such as at the built-in wardrobe in the master bedroom or at the low table in the living area. In both of the bedrooms, a bench and shelving composition has been installed at the windows. Lined with cushions, it provides a restful niche with a pleasant view to the surroundings. A "sculptural" bar counter is the only divider between the kitchen and the living space. The custom-made kitchen cabinets are designed in spray paint finish with horizontal shadow lines throughout.

DISSOLVING THE BOX

house at bukit antarabangsa

Alterations to an existing house of "Modernist" extraction have struck a balance between comfort, practicality and aesthetic value.

PROJECT LOCATION **BUKIT ANTARABANGSA, MALAYSIA**
ARCHITECT/DESIGNER **RICHARD SE/PH+D DESIGN**
PHOTOGRAPHER **RICHARD SE**
TEXT **RICHARD SE**

The original house is one of the 120 units in a 12 year-old estate designed by Malaysian architect Ken Yeang. It is a very simple concrete structure in a "Modern" style, with two courtyards to take advantage of natural lighting and ventilation. One of the courtyards next to the kitchen had been roofed over by the previous residents.

The client wanted to increase the living and dining areas. The designers opened up the view to the garden and hills at the rear of the house where the dining and the living rooms are located. Existing brick walls were replaced with floor-to-ceiling glass doors for unobstructed views out to the rear. A small outdoor terrace was created at the adjoining space between the living and the dining room. It is sheltered witha clear polycarbonate roof and a fine bamboo screen, converting this area into a breezy and shady space that is particularly enjoyable in the evenings. With the walls around "dissolved", the living area and its terraces are now visually and physically extended into the garden and beyond.

The entrance foyer was tiled with terracotta and to further define this part of the house, all the main interior areas of the ground floor were raised in a warm red razak timber platform. New ceilings for this floor were designed to accommodate recessed lighting features that enhanced the spaces. Decorative water features, in the form of a shallow pond at the entrance, were introduced to create a calming effect. A low timber wall doubles as a seat for guests. The elaborate main door serves as a contrast to the subtle design of the house. The end result is that the design strikes a balance between comfort, practicality, and aesthetic value.

WITHIN AND WITHOUT

timber house at batu laut

The penetrable exterior of vernacular Malaysian domestic architecture is further dematerialised in this house, where the dining, living and private areas are divided into three pavilions, and baths are located in the open air.

PROJECT LOCATION **BATU LAUT, SELANGOR, MALAYSIA**
ARCHITECT/DESIGNER **C'ARCH ARCHITECTURE + DESIGN SDN BHD**
PHOTOGRAPHER **GERALD LOPEZ, AHMAD SABKI**
TEXT **RICHARD SE**

The 3.5 acre site is a typically Malay orchard, cocooned by the vastness of the sea, a delicate belt of mangrove, the village cemetery and some artificially created ponds. The house itself consists of three clusters of separate but linked pavilions. These are reminiscent of traditional Malaysian domestic architecture, with their mostly stilted timber structure, extensive openings and wide eaves and verandahs. These vernacular Malaysian building techniques are of course perfectly suited to the tropical climate, and here they provide a delightful living environment that allows cooling ventilation and a soft filtered light.

The first of the clusters contains the dining space. It is surrounded by gardens and water features, which provide both a physical and visual engagement with the site. The living pavilion, which is opposite the dining pavilion, is raised off the ground and encompasses the formal entrance to the house. An opening in the living space cluster reveals a bridge, which spans a small garden. This bridge connects the living space with the bedrooms and study pavilion. This third pavilion is detached from the public spaces and enjoys the intimacy of luxurious open baths set in private gardens.

The building envelope is somewhat indistinct in this type of climatically driven architecture. Shutters can be opened up, dissolving walls. Wide verandahs become extensions of internal rooms, and are adorned with furniture. The designers of this house have further augmented the concept of outdoor living by dividing the house into distinct pavilions (requiring the occupants to physically exit the enclosures and re-enter), and by locating baths outside in the open air. Life in this house is as much within as without.

COMPARE AND CONTRAST

commonwealth
avenue west

The designers at Wide Open Spaces have echoed their company name in the refurbishment of this apartment for a young couple, with a neutral backdrop punctuated by joinery and sculptural furniture.

PROJECT LOCATION **COMMONWEALTH AVENUE WEST, SINGAPORE**
FLOOR AREA **1600SQFT**
ARCHITECT/DESIGNER **GAYLE LEONG, DAPHNE ANG/WIDE OPEN SPACES**
PHOTOGRAPHER **KELLEY CHENG**
TEXT **NARELLE YABUKA**

The perceived floor area of this 3-bedroom Housing Development Board (HDB) apartment has been maximised with plentiful windows, a neutral treatment of floors and walls, and screens that allow visual penetration between rooms. A feeling of airiness has been created, with maximum light transmission into and through the interior by way of frosted glass doors.

The palette of materials used is modest, even austere - there is a cement screed floor in the living areas, the walls are painted in a pale fawn-brown, and dark timber architectural features divide and define spaces. The palette is simple, but the contrast between the elements is striking. Clutter is non-existent. Instead, sparsely arranged, sculptural items of furniture, highlighted by halogen downlights, join forces with the timber elements to punctuate the space. Meanwhile, light brings the details alive; when light hits the screed floor for example, it comes alive through its texture.

The timber elements have been designed with a high level of detail. The timber strip-screen that greets you at the entrance has been detailed so that it can be pulled out from its position to allow furniture to be easily moved in and out of the apartment. The bar counter fronting the kitchen has a folding wire-glass, timber framed shutter to impede cooking smells from penetrating the living area. Dark timber laminated cupboards in the kitchen match the other joinery throughout the rest of the apartment. Stainless steel on the kitchen benches provides a visually strong contrast to the dominant timber. The master bedroom encompasses the study area, which is separated from the dining room by a double-sided timber shelving unit.

ARTFUL ARRANGEMENT

figaro street house

Singaporean artist and designer Michael Cu Fua's house is testament to his design sensibilities for a modern tropical house - clean, simple and functional, celebratory of the natural climate, with a refined yet casual approach.

PROJECT LOCATION **FIGARO STREET, SINGAPORE**
FLOOR AREA **1500SQFT**
ARCHITECT/DESIGNER **MICHAEL CU FUA/CU FUA ASSOCIATES**
PHOTOGRAPHER **THE PRESS ROOM**
TEXT **NARELLE YABUKA**

Designing a house for oneself is the biggest challenge that any designer faces. Designing requires an understanding of the client and their needs, and understanding yourself as a client is not easy. So Cu Fua engaged the services of his wife as the "client" to critique his scheme for their terrace house in Figaro Street. The result is a space that has the semi-unkempt charm of a male artist, moderated by female sensibility.

A defining design element that made it through the critique process - just - is the black floor: a monolithic base stretching from the front porch to the rear dining area. It extends beyond glass partitions, and spatially blows out the front and rear boundaries of the intimately sized terrace house. Black has been an important colour in Cu Fua's paintings. He used it heavily in his earlier works as part of his quest for independence. These early works were often devoid of backgrounds, thanks to his generous use of black. In his own home, the black floor is like a canvas for living on.

Another feature is the enclosure, or lack thereof, of the bedroom. It opens unabashedly into the living room, enclosed only by sliding glass partitions and curtains that can be drawn in sheepish moments. However, such a lack of visual segregation was not an exercise in exhibitionism or voyeurism; the intention was to alleviate claustrophobic spatial restrictions. The glass partitions exist primarily to keep the air-conditioning in, rather than prying eyes out.

DRAW THE LINE

fortredale apartment

Spatial restraint is often a problem in apartments. Moveable horizontal and vertical screens have been employed in this Fortredale condominium apartment to create expansive lines of sight and give spaces a dual function.

PROJECT LOCATION **FORT ROAD, SINGAPORE**
FLOOR AREA **1600SQFT**
ARCHITECT/DESIGNER **WHIZ CONCEPTS**
PHOTOGRAPHER **KELLEY CHENG**
TEXT **NARELLE YABUKA**

The designers were asked to create more space within the boundary of the apartment. In the original plan, the apartment was compartmentalised into 3 bedrooms, a living-cum-dining area, a kitchen and other utilities. The spaces were lamentably tight. In an effort to increase spaciousness, one of the bedrooms was merged with the adjacent master bedroom, and the dining area has been brought into the kitchen space, freeing up the living area.

Visual strategies were also used to increase feelings of spaciousness. This approach is best illustrated by the series of white strip-screens that run the entire length of the living, dining and kitchen spaces. These screens draw the eye through the space, creating a continuous flow of visual rhythm, and camouflaging various utilitarian objects - such as the television, kitchen sink and stovetop - along the way. The manipulation of these operable screens transforms the dining room into the kitchen, and the corridor into the living room, and vice versa. They are an ingenious means of saving space, by applying a dual function to rooms.

Reflective surfaces have been included to contrast and complement the visual permeability of the strip-screens. The custom-made, moveable stainless steel backrests to the marble dining bench serve to reflect the panoramic views from the apartment, as well as to break the horizontality of the strip-screens and dining bench. A mirrored wall at one end of the living area echoes the design of the entire space, amplifying imagined spaciousness.

HOUSE CLEANING

ghim moh flat

Clean lines within an expanse of interconnected space define this soothing environment for relaxation. The "house cleaning" process of the renovation has changed the original layout through elimination, reconstruction and a tinge of innovation.

PROJECT LOCATION **GHIM MOH, SINGAPORE**
FLOOR AREA **1240SQFT**
ARCHITECT/DESIGNER **WHIZ CONCEPTS**
PHOTOGRAPHER **KELLEY CHENG**
TEXT **NARELLE YABUKA**

The apartment was given a total makeover, with design, demolition and construction taking place within a short period of just 4 months. The cleaning up and restructuring of spaces, which eliminated all redundant elements and injected new basic contemporary components, has resulted in a bright, simple and airy space.

The whitewashed walls, white ceramic tiles and beech flooring used throughout create an environment of calm and appeasement. The design concept proposed that the furniture and other fittings should visually complement the rest of the interior, and not create vast contrasts and visual protrusions. Cream-coloured seating and tables blend quietly with the interior's envelope. Frosted glass sliding doors, softly transmitting light, further reflect the idea of calm and repose that had been sought. Clarity and uniformity is reinforced by the creation of recesses and wall niches to store the television, and to display decorative items.

Mirrors are employed for visual enhancement of the space. They are particularly effective on a raised niche in the ceiling of the dining room; here, they take on the appearance of a skylight, and significantly lighten the room with their reflection of white and light. A timber ledge along one wall in the dining room acts as both a display shelf and as a punctuation mark in the enveloping white interior.

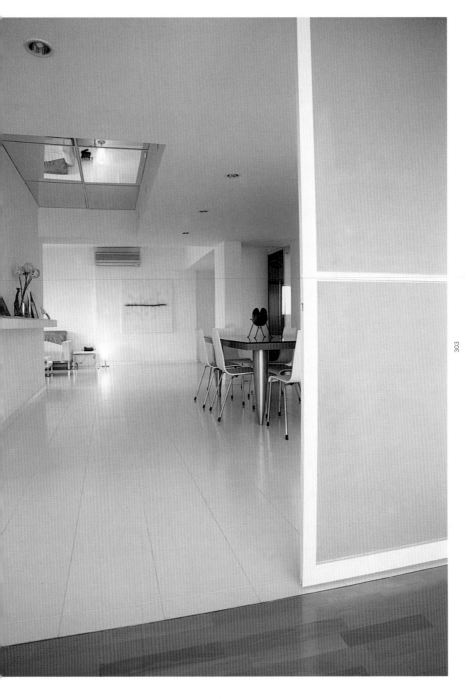

DESIGN BY INTUITION

house at
jalan bahagia

Playful and eclectic, this terrace house for two architects abates rhetoric in favour of direct and surprising expression.

PROJECT LOCATION **JALAN BAHAGIA, SINGAPORE**
ARCHITECT/DESIGNER **RANDY CHAN, JANCY RAHARDJA/ZONG ARCHITECTS**
PHOTOGRAPHER **KELLEY CHENG**
TEXT **NARELLE YABUKA**

Randy Chan and Jancy Rahardja are budget-conscious urbanites with a penchant for good design. Randy is an artist as well as an architect. The passionate methods which he uses to create his installation artworks involve situating objects in a way that he cannot always explain. His wife, Jancy, is also an architect, whose work springs from a much more pragmatic viewpoint. Together, as Zong Architects, they achieve a balanced design approach.

The couple wanted their house to be a place where they could step back from their daily work and reflect. They wanted to be able to have their individual space within the house and they wanted it to be easily maintained. But perhaps of most importance was that the creation of their home would be a low budget affair. Their approach to the design of the renovations was that every line on the drawing attributes to cost. It is fortunate that they wanted a fairly open, uncluttered space. But in fact, some unique features in the house happened as a result of constraints.

A lot of the things in this house are low-cost, D-I-Y creations. For example, in the front entrance area, they chose not to rip up the existing pink floor tiles, but instead they just laid "geotextile", loose pebble-wash stones and a few granite slabs. The unconventional perforated metal screen on the street facade is a device for mediation between the public and private. It keeps out the direct rays of the sun, and at the same time, it filters the views of the neighbourhood. The fun and liberty that the couple took when designing their home has provided them with a playful and inspiring environment in which there is room to think.

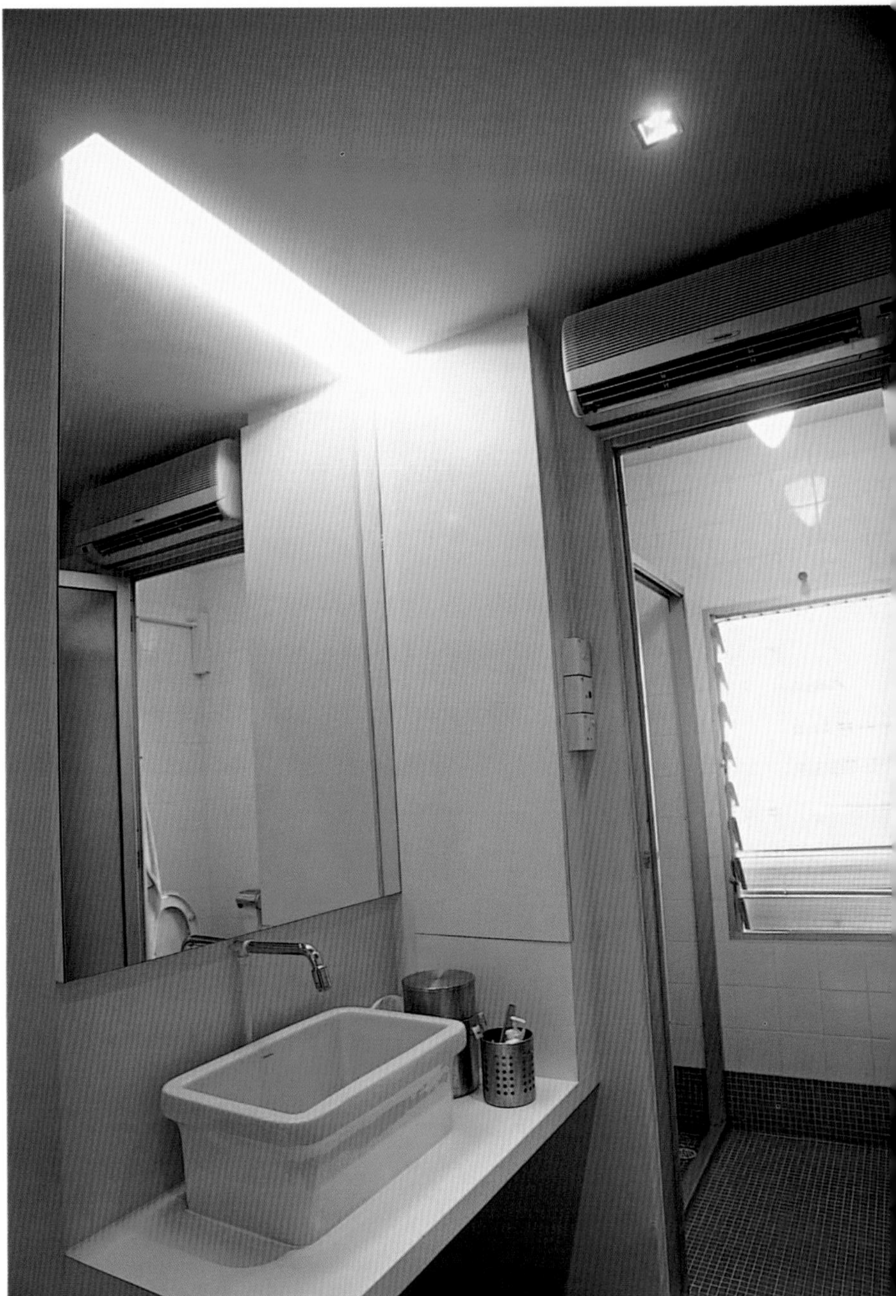

ART AND MONASTICISM

kim tian road apartment

Ethereal and surreal, raw and abstract, this Kim Tian Road apartment combines the spatial qualities of a gallery with the restraint of a monastery to create a space of both exhibitionism and reductionism.

PROJECT LOCATION **KIM TIAN ROAD, SINGAPORE**
FLOOR AREA **1200SQFT**
ARCHITECT/DESIGNER **WHIZ CONCEPTS**
PHOTOGRAPHER **KELLEY CHENG**
TEXT **NARELLE YABUKA**

The beauty of this scheme is that the apartment has literally been transformed into a piece of art itself, raising questions like any powerful piece of art would. The interior is composed of three layers: a layer of cement screed on the floor, a layer of black-painted elements, and a layer of white walls and ceilings enveloping the spaces. A striking 7.4 metre plane of solid timber flanked by black mild steel benches forms the spatial and visual centerpiece of the apartment. Function-specific furniture such as sofas and chairs are absent. Instead, custom-designed furniture such as the timber structure, a row of polyurethane foam, and concrete platforms provide open-ended interpretations for the users to explore and define the function.

Much attention has been given to detailing. The best illustration of this is a specially-designed screen that conceals the television. Clad in fabric, the screen glides open and closed to reveal and conceal the television set. Even within utilitarian areas such as the kitchen and bathroom, the aesthetics have been worked to the smallest detail to build up the austere sense of a gallery or monastery. A "black hole" defines the kitchen, which is a stark ensemble of a cement screed worktop set within a black niche in the wall. The bathroom features a concrete sink that builds upon the idea of a waterfall.

This is an apartment that requires of its occupants a degree of strength and confidence. There is nowhere to hide, but it is a feat of ingenuity and discipline. And really, we all secretly want to be exhibitionists, don't we? With its seemingly unwelcoming palette of cement and black steel, the space echoes with a cold austerity that is antithetical to the archetypal image of a home. In fact, it seems more like an art installation or a monastery than a living space.

BLANK CANVAS

lengkong tiga apartment

Whiz Concepts gave this HDB apartment in Lengkong Tiga a "twist of simplicity" by cleverly incorporating trendy understated design language. Its straightforward yet unique character is tailored specifically to the needs of the occupants.

PROJECT LOCATION **LENGKONG TIGA, SINGAPORE**
FLOOR AREA **1090SQFT**
ARCHITECT/DESIGNER **WHIZ CONCEPTS**
PHOTOGRAPHER **KELLEY CHENG**
TEXT **NARELLE YABUKA**

For Maria and her daughter, their ideal living space is one that is stylish, simple and practical. Carefully avoiding the term "minimalism", Maria's brief was merely the request for the creation of a straightforward and practical design that would be simple to maintain and easy to clean. With little opportunity to cook at home, Maria had requested that the kitchen be kept nifty and simple. Besides these basic requirements, the rest was left to the ingenuity of the designers of the project, Whiz Concepts.

Left without the need to install the usual wall-consuming cabinets, the designers seized the opportunity to make the island counter the focus of the kitchen and practically the highlight of the apartment. The sleek counter was also designed to replace the dining table that is conventionally the best representation of a family. The absence of it hints at the fast-moving lifestyles of the inhabitants.

With the designers' use of clean lines, a strong but limited palette of materials and well-resolved angles and details, the spatial expression of the rest of the apartment is one that is fluid, simple and elegant. To Maria, a simple design and a straightforward layout is certainly more than just a fad. It is a preferred way of life. Whiz Concepts have provided a blank canvas for the occupants, upon which they can subsequently live and decorate as they please.

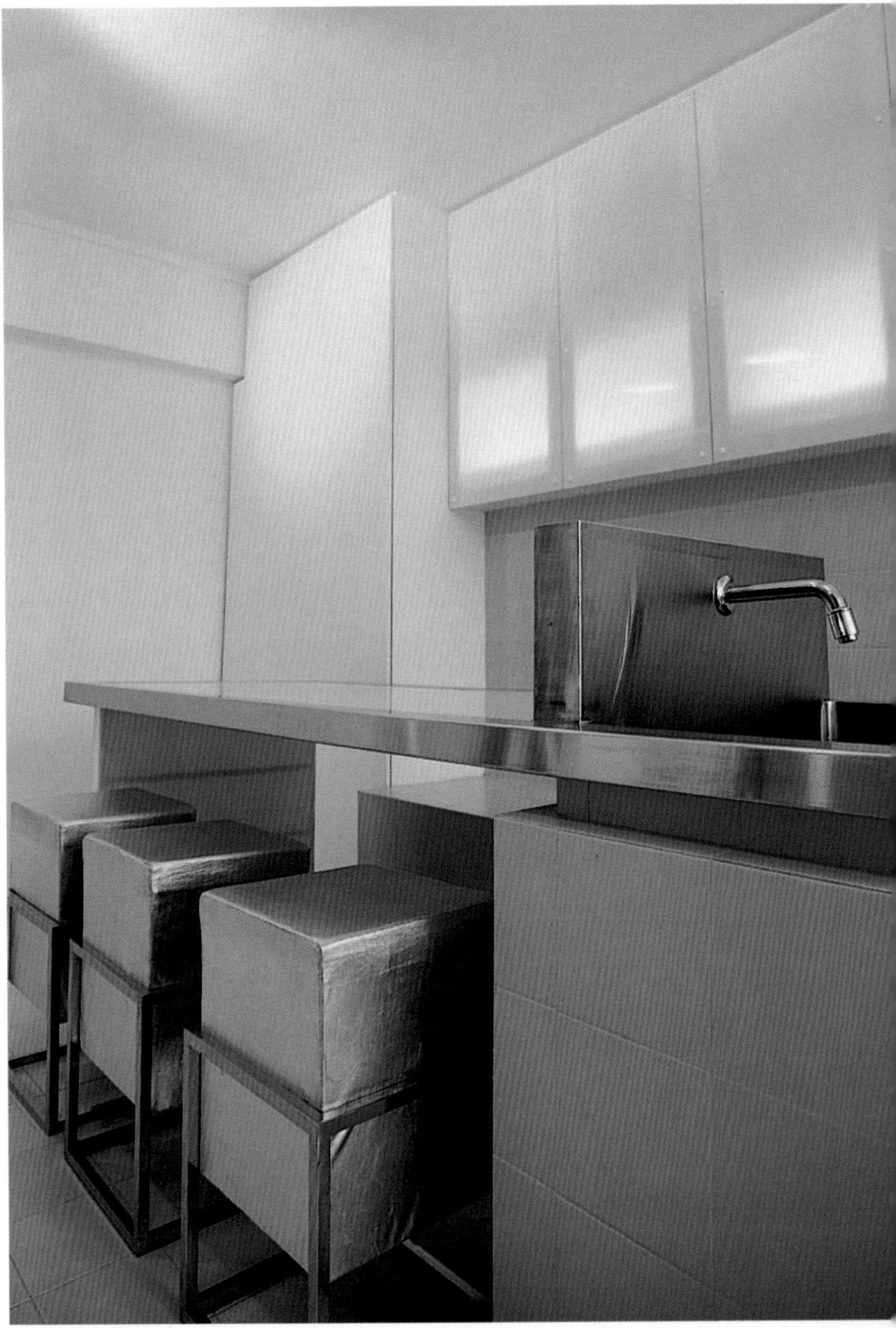

BREATHING LIGHT

moulmein road apartment

The physical form and delicate poetic capacity of the lantern have been translated into liveable space, which breathes light and advocates the philosophical.

PROJECT LOCATION **MOULMEIN ROAD, SINGAPORE**
FLOOR AREA **1200SQFT**
ARCHITECT/DESIGNER **BENJAMIN KIM/THE MATCHBOX**
PHOTOGRAPHER **KELLEY CHENG**
TEXT **NARELLE YABUKA**

The lantern bears a strong architectonic quality that has long inspired the design of many artefacts. Enclosed within its rigid frame is not only a volume of space from which light is emitted, but also a great poetic capacity. The Moulmein Road Apartment is much like several lanterns melded together and transformed into liveable space. Skins of clear and frosted glass, breathing light in all manners - sharp, gentle, bright and soft - weave around the apartment with timber planes, carving space and directing the eye.

The ribbed timber and glass composition that encloses the master bedroom, inspired by a traditional paper lantern, forms a focal point in the narrow living/dining space. It captures the eye and coaxes attention away from the long linear stretch of space. When the bedroom is illuminated, a soft, seductive glow radiates through this lantern wall, and the public areas of the apartment resonate with pure lightness. Complementing this lantern, is an assemblage of timber cladding and sliding doors, which wrap the walls of the master bedroom.

The delicate beauty of the scheme resides in the sensual play of light without the use of radical strategies. Alternating between bright and dark, and weaving quietly around the space with timber and glass, light practically becomes a tangible material in this minimal and delightful apartment.

INVISIBLE LIVING

oxley rise apartment

Designed by Weave Interior for a music lover, this loft apartment has been transformed into an open space with distinct elements, inspired by the spatial music of Harold Budd and Brian Eno.

PROJECT LOCATION **OXLEY RISE, SINGAPORE**
FLOOR AREA **1100SQFT**
ARCHITECT/DESIGNER **BRENDA NG/WEAVE INTERIOR**
PHOTOGRAPHER **TERENCE YEUNG**

Like the reverberating spaces between the distinct notes in Budd's and Eno's compositions, this loft is conceptualised as an open space with distinct fixed elements. Using only a limited palette of materials in the design of the studio space, a dark brown, compressed-ply music centrepiece is held in a taut textual juxtaposition by the light-grey natural cement screed walls that surround it. White drapes, floating surreally, conceal the storage racks and help balance the boxy brown wooden closet opposite the bed. Daily essentials are deliberately hidden from the eye in cleverly designed storage spaces, achieving what the owner calls "invisible living". This visual elimination results in an interior space that focuses on real living, and not on mundane existence created by the accumulation of excesses.

The bathroom is perhaps the most distinctive element of the interior. Visually connected to the bedroom, but spatially divided by a glass wall, the spacious bathroom emphasises the concept of purification through the ritual of bathing. Privacy from the neighbours is provided by the green foliage of a big tree just outside. Consistent with the rest of the loft, the bathroom has been deconstructed into distinct elements such as the prominent free-standing washbasin and the architectonic bath.

All these new paradigms for living have been introduced because of what both the owner and designer wished to create - a reorientation of daily life. The owner was seeking purification from the visually exhausting urban experience. The music-cum-living space, continuously connected to the kitchen, attempts to reveal the energetic experimentation of the owner by fusing two disparate activities simultaneously in day-to-day living.

A PLOT FOR CONTEMPLATION

punggol road apartment

Plots and sub-plots compose this writer's apartment, with space sufficient and conducive to thought, contemplation and composition.

PROJECT LOCATION **PUNGGOL ROAD, SINGAPORE**
FLOOR AREA **1200SQFT**
ARCHITECT/DESIGNER **MICHAEL CU FUA/CU FUA ASSOCIATES**
PHOTOGRAPHER **KELLEY CHENG**
TEXT **NARELLE YABUKA**

This is an apartment for a freelance writer who works from home. The designer, a close friend, was given free reign to design of his own accord, the only constraint being a low budget. He has created two stories in the apartment; one is a story of enveloping brightness, the other of accentuating darkness. The white walls, floor, ceiling and sofa in the living room are punctuated by dark timber elements - loose furniture (coffee table, sideboard, dining setting, bookcase), and built-in cabinetry. These concealed cupboards are of a deceiving appearance; they are detailed to be deceptively thin at the edge.

There are sliding glass doors to the balcony, allowing maximum access to inspirational views and light, and the opportunity for the balcony to be opened up as an extension of the living room. An intimate interior scale has been given to the balcony, with niches in the walls for the purpose of holding potted plants. Wall niches are included inside too, and provide another layer of focal points in the sea of white.

The pattern of dark focal elements in a field of light is repeated in the bedroom and bathroom. But the bathroom is defined as another zone entirely - like a sub-plot in the main story - by way of intricate blue mosaic tiling in two shades, on the walls, floor and bench. But the timber elements still manage to interject, as dark stripes of joinery and an overhead beam. Dark timber closets punctuate the airy bedroom.

A BOX WITHIN A BOX

telok blangah apartment

The idea of a box within a box is manifested in this 3-bedroom HDB apartment at Telok Blangah Heights, designed by practicing architect-owners, Warren Liu and Darlene Smyth.

PROJECT LOCATION **TELOK BLANGAH ROAD, SINGAPORE**
FLOOR AREA **1240SQFT**
ARCHITECT/DESIGNER **WARREN LIU, DARLENE SMITH**
PHOTOGRAPHER **RIDA SOBANA/COURTESY OF WARREN LIU**
TEXT **NARELLE YABUKA**

To Warren and Darlene, the design of their own apartment was grounds for the experimentation and realisation of ideas that would otherwise have been impossible in the commercial projects that they take on at work. The couple was concerned with the programmatic aspects of their design. As Warren put it, "We wanted a big room, a big room with a lot of flexibility." Deeming it too wasteful to compartmentalise space as in the original plan, they decided to open up the spaces by removing most of the internal walls and reconfiguring the layout. In their words, they wanted to test how events and activities, rather than form, would shape space.

The main idea is that of a box with a permeable shell within another box. The external shell of the flat is the enclosing outer "box". The inner box is conceptualised as a flexible unit that has the capabilities to transform according to changing needs. A permeable skin surrounding this inner box defines a transitory space between the external shell and the innermost unit. Light and air are allowed to filter through the spaces while maintaining visual and contextual linkages.

Three layers of spaces have been created in a rich palette of warm colours, textures of timber, cream walls and cement screed. The first layer consists of the inner box, which exists as a concealed "study alcove" set back-to-back with a row of wardrobes, which also form part of the master bedroom enclosure. The second layer consists of a screen of timber posts set around the inner box, embodying the main circulation path within the apartment. In the third layer, neutral spaces, partitioned using structural columns, have been formulated. These spaces, regular in plan and homogeneous in quality, can be freely adapted to various uses according to requirements.

MAGNIFICENTLY MACHINED

ban suan saghob

Inspired by Mies and machines, this architect's house takes cues from the International Style, but its expression is entirely vernacular.

PROJECT LOCATION **BANGKOK, THAILAND**
PHOTOGRAPHER **SOMKID PAIMPIYACHAT/SKYLINE STUDIO**
ARCHITECT/DESIGNER **PRABHAKORN VADANYAKUL/ARCHITECTS 49 LIMITED**
TEXT **SAVINEE BURANASILAPIN & THOMAS DANNECKER**

Prabhakorn Vadanyakul has a machine in his garden. An airplane, to be exact. The architect has had a lifelong obsession with all things mechanical, and airplanes in particular. He has been building models for as long as he can remember, and has been a private pilot for a decade. It comes as no surprise that his own house exhibits a stunning complexity of detail and craftsmanship. What surprises visitors is how flawlessly it is integrated with its environment - a lush, wooded site outside of Bangkok. "I want to show that nature and technology are not polar issues," says Vadanyakul.

Aspects of his house read like a subtler version of its modernist ancestor, Mies van der Rohe's Farnsworth House. Where Mies made an empty glass box with a service core in the middle, Vadanyakul has stacked up three of Mies' boxes, altered their sizes according to function, and started detailing. He added sunshades, water protection, acoustic isolation, privacy screens, and the occasional airplane-influenced part, like the section of a stair tread or a door. Every extreme that nature exposes the house to is incorporated into the technology of the house. Where Farnsworth House quickly proved itself unliveable due to its exposure to weather and prying neighbours, Vadhankul's house uses its trees for privacy, the rain to fill its cooling pool and supplement its shower, and the sun (filtered) for light, even in the core. His glass is operable to an extreme degree - an entire wall pivots to expose the dining room to an outdoor terrace and pool.

Mies-inspired details crop up here and there: in the cantilever of a bed from its headboard, in the celebration of a steel column penetrating the floor, in an imperceptible threshold between indoors and out. But this house does not bear the pretence of the "International Style" - it can only exist exactly where it is.

UNWITTINGLY WONDERFUL

beaux house

Designer instincts saved this little house from demolition, and saw it transformed into a split-level playground for a family of three.

PROJECT LOCATION **BANGKOK, THAILAND**
ARCHITECT/DESIGNER **PICHAI-THEERANUJ WONGWAISAYAWAN**
PHOTOGRAPHER **KELLEY CHENG**
TEXT **SAVINEE BURANASILAPIN & THOMAS DANNECKER**

When the husband/wife - architect/designer team of Pichai and Theeranuj Wongwaisayawan bought this tiny house in Bangkok, their initial intent was to renovate it just enough to be comfortable while they waited to find the time to tear it down and build a new house. But they could not resist their designer instincts. Renovations became increasingly radical, and they find themselves, somewhat unwittingly, in an unusual home but which suits their lifestyle, and their 7 year-old daughter, just fine.

Where the old house was a pile of tiny rooms on two floors, demolishing several key interior walls has turned it an interior landscape of level changes, partial-height walls, and built-in furniture. It is a playground of unpredictable nooks, crannies, and shared surfaces. The ground floor is an interconnected series of small living spaces, on three levels, which wrap around a central staircase. Each level extends beyond the house to form an exterior deck, two of which share a stair with their interior counterparts. The upper floor is on two levels, on either side of the staircase. First is a child's room with bath and a spare living space, which can be closed off to form a guest bedroom. The uppermost level holds the master bedroom suite, which is arranged in a linear sequence: dressing, closet, bathroom.

The decorating scheme owes a lot to American kitsch, which to the designer-owners is a welcome relief. Since they both work for the same major firm, known for its clean "modern" designs, they are happy to leave their work behind in search of something more uniquely theirs. What they have found is something that has largely been left out of the orthodox modern canon - the spatially attenuated interiors of Adolf Loos.

DESIGN BY FUSION

gerd fabritius condo

Cross-cultural Asian motifs meet head on with high-end technological touches in this hybridised apartment for an expatriate living in Bangkok.

PROJECT LOCATION **BANGKOK, THAILAND**
ARCHITECT/DESIGNER **RUJIRAPORN PIA WANGLEE/P INTERIOR & ASSOCIATES CO., LTD.**
PHOTOGRAPHER **SKYLINE STUDIO**
TEXT **SAVINEE BURANASILAPIN & THOMAS DANNECKER**

If European Modernist architecture counts traditional Asian architecture among its ancestors, and contemporary Asian architecture counts American Post-Modernist architecture among its ancestors, what are we to make of this contemporary Bangkok condominium for a European expatriate, by an Asian architect, which uses cross-cultural, pan-Asian motifs with high-end technological touches? The cultural-historical issues are many, but the material consequences are noteworthy, as well.

An open plan allows natural light through balcony doors on opposite sides of the building. The main living space, which could easily be lost in the darkness of the building's wide floor plate, is thus turned into a hovering plane of polished wooden floorboards between 2 window walls, loosely divided into rooms by furniture and screens. A home office opens onto the main space, but can be enclosed by extravagantly detailed sliding translucent screens, a Japanese touch with just a bit of British high-tech.

Bedrooms and bathrooms fill out the balcony-lined corners of the plan. One is a guest bedroom, tucked away behind the office and a powder room. The other, more prominent by far, is the master bedroom. It is entered past a massive pivoting circle of glass, precisely engineered to mate with a circular punched opening, borrowed from traditional Chinese architecture. At the opposite end of the master bedroom, a blind corner grants privacy to a bathroom. Rather, it is a bath hall, terminated by a dramatic washbasin, lined with infinite reflections of mirror-clad closet and shower doors. A miniature indoor Zen garden breaks the monotony on one side, with a European-style water closet planted among its stones - a slightly surreal symbol of Bangkok architecture's pedigree.

388

CLARITY OF FORM

osataphan residence

In recent years, Chiangmai, the cultural capital of northern Thailand, has been heavily influenced by the building traditions of the region's past, with its interiors often attempting to evoke traditional teakwood houses. The boldness and modernity of the Osataphan residence make it an especially striking inclusion to the region.

PROJECT LOCATION CHIANGMAI, THAILAND
ARCHITECT/DESIGNER ARCHITECTS 49 LIMITED/IA ARCHITECTS 49 LIMITED
PHOTOGRAPHER SKYLINE STUDIO
TEXT SAVINEE BURANASILAPIN & THOMAS DANNECKER

The Osataphan residence is a thoroughly modern piece of architecture - a surgically clean white box with an interior that looks not to the romanticised past, but to the landscape that surrounds it. It brings to mind Mies van der Rohe's minimalist collages, where an interior is represented as nothing more than the view from its windows and an art object that it contains. While IA49's interior demonstrates a Miesian relationship with the landscape, it is certainly not Miesian in its details.

Rooms are clearly demarcated by thick walls with punched-out door openings. The ceiling reinforces functional boundaries, with a rectangular plane hovering above each space. Recessed lights and window shades preserve the clarity of the form of the house. In the living and dining rooms, the ceiling is reduced to a thin frame around the room's perimeter, defining a human-scaled ceiling height, but opening to a generous clerestory above, which admits natural light.

Underfoot, a warm wooden floor unites the sequence of rooms. Flowing uninterrupted between them, it occasionally reaches upwards to encompass a piece of interior trim or cabinetry, stopping only when it reaches the envelope of glass and aluminum that (barely) encloses this space as an interior. Iconic furniture and objets d'art are arrayed upon the flowing floor plane, rounding out this picture of Modernism, retouched for contemporary Chiangmai.

architects' email index

AUSTRALIA

Nicholas Gioia, Rodger Smith, Nicholas Dour, Patrick
Gilfedder/Nicholas Gioia Architects
alexas@bigpond.com

Shelley Penn/Shelley Penn Architects
sjpenn@bigpond.com

HONG KONG

AB Concept Ltd
info@abconcept.com.hk

Andre Fu/AFSO Design
afsodesign@aol.com

BHI Ltd
bruce.harwood@bhi-group.com

Draughtzman
allyoop@netvigator.com

Dillon Garris
dillongarris@aol.com

Chang/Edge (HK) Ltd
edgeltd@netvigator.com

Jason Caroline Design Ltd
jas_car@hotmail.com

KplusK Associates
kplusk@netvigator.com

Frank Chiu/ONE: China Studio
one@netvigator.com

Sunaqua Concepts Ltd
sunaqua@hkstar.com

MALAYSIA

C'arch Architecture + Design Sdn Bhd
carch@myjaring.net

Richard Se/Ph+D Design
phd_design@mac.com

Susanne Zeidler, Ng Kien Teck/ZLG Sdn Bhd
zlg@pd.jaring.my

SINGAPORE

Michael Cu Fua/Cu Fua Associates
cufua@pacific.net.sg

Benjamin Kim/The Matchbox
benjamin@the-matchbox.com

Brenda Ng/Weave Interior
weave@singnet.com

Whiz Concepts
whizcon@cyberway.com.sg

Gayle Leong, Daphne Ang/Wide Open Spaces
wos@swiftech.net.sg

Randy Chan, Jancy Rahardja/Zong Architects
zongarch@singnet.com.sg

THAILAND

Architects 49 Limited
a49@49group.com

IA Architects 49 Limited
ia49@49group.com

Prabhakorn Vadanyakul/Architects 49 Limited
prabhakorn@aa49.com

Rujiraporn PIA Wangle/P Interior & Associates Co Ltd
pia@pia-group.com

Pichai-Theeranuj Wongwaisayawan
bonoi@loxinfo.co.th

acknowledgement

We would like to thank all the architects, designers for their kind permission to publish their works; all the photographers who have generously granted us permission to use their images; all our foreign co-ordinators – Anna Koor, Barbara Cullen, Kwah Meng-Ching, Reiko Kasai, Richard Se, Savinee Buranasilapin, Tatsuo Iso, Thomas Dannecker for their hard work and invaluable help; and most of all, to all the homeowners who have so graciously allowed us to photograph their beautiful homes and to share them with readers the world over. Also, thank you to all those who have helped in one way or another in putting together this book.

Thank you all.